A
POTPOURRI
OF
PROSE AND POETRY

From

The Chestertown (KCPL) Writers
Group

Little Bear Press
Chestertown, MD

A Potpourri of Prose and Poetry
Copyright © 2013
The Chestertown Writers Group
All rights reserved
ISBN-13: 978-0615903200

Little Bear Press.
448 Pear Tree Point Road, Chestertown. MD 21620

Dedication

To the
Kent County Public Library for
Sponsoring
our Writers Group
and with
a special "Thank You"
to
Karin Cowperthwait
Who started it all.

CONTENTS

CONTENTS *continued*

DINING OUT
By: Alice Lindsay

"Right this way, Mrs. Lindsay."

"Thank you, Pierre," I answer.

My husband and I follow the maître d' to the candlelit, more or less secluded table in a quiet corner of my favorite restaurant. I am relaxed, content and into reading the menu.

It isn't always that way with me when dining out. I once swatted flies with my shoe in a supposedly upscale New York eatery. But, no, as a rule it's the tables that bug me.

I am convinced maître d's everywhere have it in for me. I wouldn't be surprised if they have my name on their worst tables holding them in reserve at all times in case I show up. Call it paranoia, but let the facts speak for themselves.

Leaving aside the many Charlie Chaplin poor-soul seating arrangements next to squeaky swinging doors leading out to kitchens, take the table just under the room air conditioner in the home style cooking truck stop: an ancient, rusty leviathan of an air cooler protrudes precariously out of a jagged hole in the wall just above my table. Taped all around the edges with cruddy duck-tape that's peeling off in loose dangling strips, it hums, rattles, belches and vibrates, while dripping water, Chinese water torture style, down one rusty side onto my table.

I consider pulling the plug stuck in the outlet just above my left shoulder as I survey the lunch hour crowd of beer swilling, hot sweaty Teamsters. I dare to reach up to turn the temperature dial to 'low' but jerk back my arm at the gruff snarl:

"Hey, lady, what the hell ya think yer doin?"

And that was one of the friendlier looking truckers.

Okay, so you ask, "What is she doing eating in a truck stop?" I'm here because I'm having lunch with my son. He's a freshman at college. He says I'll love the chili. I remind him he shouldn't believe all that garbage about truck drivers knowing all the good places to eat. But then his grandfather *is* a Teamster, and, yes, the chili is delicious.

Then there's that table in too many restaurants-the one smack in the middle of all the other tables in the room, the one with a precarious marriage and two rotten kids:

"George kicked me, Mom!"

"I did not."

"Stop kicking Harold, George."

"They're only playing, Marie."

"And how would you know, Mr. Never-at-Home with the kids."

"I just thought . . ."

"Oh, just shut up."

Or there's the two tables pushed together for the office party of eight drunks singing, "Happy Birthday, Vera!" and "For She's a Jolly Good Office Manager . . ." amid a pile of joke gifts and helium balloons.

Meanwhile waiters and busboys balancing trays of dinners and dirty dishes go rushing around my table in

2

a swirling dervish, bumping my chair, brushing my back and dropping food. I'm still finding bits of Thousand Island dressing in a handbag I foolishly stowed on the floor beside my chair near a New York bistro birthday celebration. *Clumsy oaf!*

But it's the table next to a dirty china service station that brings out the worst in me. Take, for instance, of all places, the ritzy dining place in DC. It's our anniversary. We're dressed to the nines. We even have a reservation.

The maître d' immediately seats us at one of the many tables surrounding a spacious, elegant, polished dance floor. Not thinking it necessary, I don't case the room for bad tables and accept the maître d's choice without protest. But then I pick up on it: that unmistakable clang and clatter of plates and silverware crashing down on the service station to the rear on my right, out of the hands of a busboy taking some dissatisfaction or other out on the dishes. I wave to the maître d'.

"We'd like a different table." I announce.
Maître d' does not argue. "What table would madam like?" he asks.

I scan the possibilities. "That one, over there," I answer pointing to the other side of the room across the infinite dance floor.

Stoically, our hired host escorts us to my chosen table. I'm about to sit down, but lo and behold, I had failed to notice. There's a service cart just steps away. In fact, the infernal noisemakers are everywhere. Given the ubiquitous evil, I decide our original table is the better one.

"I guess I prefer the table we had," I say sheepishly.

"Of course, madam," replies the maître d'
without even rolling his eyes.

We start the trek back. Puzzled diners, forks full
of food suspended in mid air, follow the peripatetic party
of three traipsing once again across the dance floor. We
settle in. I thank the maître d' profusely. He nods and
departs. The waiter arrives. We order drinks and study
the menu.

"The salmon sounds good," I say in a breezy
subject-changing tone.

"You really are a control freak, you know," my
husband remarks without looking up from his menu.

"I know . . . I do need therapy . . . But, hey! Give
me *some* credit. I haven't swatted any flies, have I?"

"Not yet!" he muses.

We go back to reading the menus.

POEMS

By: Alice C. Cory

...AND REPEAT

He asks "Would you do it all again?"
But she hears "Please approve who I am."

Do it all again?
Wisdoms teach growth lies in change

If so, then
Are we ever doing it all again?

TEMPERATURE CONTROLLED

billowing, filling, sinking 'round
other's anger attacks and drowns
now all courage is tucked away
stuffed inside my frozen soul
for another day

STONE SENTINELS
(St. Paul's Churchyard Cemetery)

Endless stories cradled here
locked within their stranded stones

Families sharing chilly beds
guarded by nothingness of time

Life's signage shows bold and sharp
begging passing mortals to recall

All secrets lie within these dates
crafting chisel changed from face to fate

HOME DELIVERY
(three-word lines)

In darkness night
during meditation deep
Silent owl lands
Claws gently grasp
upon our roof
Home delivery of
inner softened peace

ENDLESS

So many beginnings
from which to choose.

It seems there are
many manies.

A few believe
there is only one,

With that one
having favored end.

But we are wiser,
aren't we.

For it is the end
that is many.

Just be careful
of all your beguns.

QUEST

I looked…
and saw it was not the seeing
but the feeling that is the sight

Finally I could feel …
and felt it was not the feeling
but the knowing that I seek

I grew to know the knowing …
and knew it was not the known
but belief for which I thirst

I believe …
and in so doing
see
and feel
and know

Oneness

COLORS OF REBIRTH

*In memory to what was, and a tribute to that which
can follow, from the mudslide at Aspen Lodge, Estes
Park, Colorado on September 12, 2013.*

Rising from the cradle of beauty and life
the black torrent rushes, claws extended wide
crushing downward, gobbling its sacrifices whole.
Human or Mother Nature, it matters not at all.

In flooding blink of cosmic eye it presses
chaotic rearrangement raining within its force
erasing much, cleaning all with oozing black swipe
then settling into deepened layer of silence.

First came the rains; soon breezes and light,
waters quieting, mud settling with promises to keep.
All returned to delicately raw beginnings,
all to the refreshed breath hidden inside earth's heart.

Green sprouts will celebrate their homecoming
finding nourishment within wild visitor's souvenirs.

But what of man? Who will arise with clearer eyes,
focus quieted, roots strengthened, grounded within
this mud?
Like fetal seedlings, yesterday's dreams re-attuned
with new footing gifted by flowing hues of change.

WITH TIME COMES...

By: Linda Garman Weimer

Time may not heal all wounds, but it does answer many of the mysteries that perplex youth. When I was a child between 8 and 11, I wondered how the older people in my family could appear content when they lived such dull lives. This perception was based only on what I saw of them, of course. The grandparents came to our small suburban house, oh, six or so times a year. The great-aunts and great-uncles joined them on the long, olive-green sofa less often-maybe once or twice a year.

This was the 1950s, which have been well documented as an era of conformity. The older women all wore dresses with flared skirts, nylons and polished shoes, the men wore suits, as if they had gone to church, which none did on the Sundays they made the trek from Philadelphia to what they considered "the country."

My mother resolutely conformed to the stereotypes of the time. My brother, sister and I had strict rules to follow on "manners," particularly saying thanks after everything done for or to us, including dental work. The rules were even stricter when we were in public; in Mom's mind, these familial visits amounted to a public presentation. As the oldest of three children, and a girl, I had warnings about keeping my legs crossed, my hair combed, standing erect, and smiling as much as possible.

A good personality and a good appearance were the requirements of successful girlhood, and soon, womanhood. This was an absolute article of faith in Mom's world.

Having grown to five feet six inches by sixth grade, I was expected to behave "like a young lady" even though I still preferred climbing trees. My brother, two years younger, would get laughs for "antics" that I would be strongly condemned for, and the youngest sibling, my sister, five years younger, was excused a lot since she was "the baby."

I felt weighed down with the burden of carrying the family's social acceptability forward. Mom's sense of responsibility in that department was so extreme that I recall, on several occasions in church, her glancing me over and then checking out the worshippers around us who had looked our way. If someone looked twice, she re-checked me. All these inspections did nothing to boost my confidence, which was predictably low.

My parents were then about 40, and the older generation in their sixties and seventies. At the big get-togethers, all the older set greeted us three kids with fondness on first sight. Then they would comment on how much or little we had grown since last visit. That was the extent of interaction in most cases.

Next, my mother, who was scurrying around in her best apron waiting for the gravy to get thick, called everyone to the dining room table, where they ate and praised her inevitable roast-beef dinner. When finished the meal, some of "the company" pushed back from the table in an apparent stupor; others repaired to the olive-green sofa.

In either location, there was little talk, unless someone of the older set had recently had, or was soon to have surgery. The news elicited nothing but mild encouragement, such as "We know how that goes."

14

And then, they proceeded to just sit there for a couple of hours more. We children were urged to hang around with them, and Mom often prompted me to talk about recent school events or ask polite questions of the generation twice removed although she never seemed to come up with anything more original than: "Ask how they are doing."

"All in all, can't complain," was the most common answer, and conversation would end again. I had no clue what they included in the first or the second "all." They seemed to have no interest in visiting my folks' garden, talking much baseball with my father or moving from their ensconced positions.

After an hour or so of this enforced presence, we kids got restless and probably annoying. So, as I recall, one of the oldsters would say, "Let them go and play." "Yeah!" my brother and sister would respond. My mother would concede, but she sent a look of frustration my way. Her oldest child had not shown sufficient personality to truly engage the guests.

The mystery to me was how the age 70 crowd could possibly be content when they did nothing, judging from what I saw.

And then it occurred to me that perhaps they were following regulations set out for them. I envisioned that, since I had to follow preteen-girl rules, they were following the precepts for their ages. I doubt if I ever wrote down their rules explicitly. But I can recall imagining that they went something like this. For those in their sixties:

1. Stop trying to amount to anything more than you are because it is too late.
2. Begin slowing down in thought, word and deed.

3. Play easy games with grandchildren, like tossing a large, soft ball, if they insist on activity.
4. Show a kindly attitude toward people as they are stronger than you and would beat you up if a disagreement arose.

The manual of dos and don'ts for those in their seventies would add:
1. Move even slower and add a hitch to your walk, so as to look stiff-jointed.
2. Avoid talking about current events and new models of cars. You probably haven't kept up with the news.
3. If you cannot hear what is being said, smile pleasantly and ignore it as the other party will repeat it if it's really important.

Now, at the time I'm describing, none of the oldsters had reached age 80 (only two would do so) but a sort of Enlightenment hit me well before that point. I don't recall exactly the year or my age, but the revelation brought just as many new questions as it answered.

It was a holiday when there was a full complement of oldsters filling the sofa and nearby swivel chairs. We kids were forced to kneel and squat on the pink and gray patterned carpet. Predictably, we were fidgeting and pushing at one another for more space. And then my paternal grandmother, usually among the quietest of the group, said with emphatic wistfulness,

"Oh, just to have some of that energy!"

And the others uttered agreements-Oh, yeses, and You said its, and That's for sures! And they uttered those remarks with more passion than I had thought them capable.

Now that I am in the oldest generation, I grasp the meaning of the remark. More arthritic than any of them, I plot and plan how to do as many small chores in one trek about the house – little things like taking shoes from the living room to the bedroom, or bringing all the condiments to the dining table on a tray in one trip.

But at the time I first heard this bit of wisdom, I was further mystified: Did it mean that these gray-haired folks still wanted to play sports and ride bikes, but somehow could not? How did they know that if they didn't try? I wondered. What, exactly, did it feel like to have no energy?

I could not recall any moments in my short life when I wanted to do something but was unable to do so due to a lack of energy, whatever that was.

Then I thought of the things my parents liked to do for fun–occasionally fox-trot in the living room to music on TV or record; go to the beach and splash in the waves in the summer; play badminton with us kids in mild weather; have social events like these Sunday dinners several times a year. Well, maybe I omitted the Sunday dinners, judging by the worried look and sharp tone of Mom's voice as she prepared for them.

Well, with such adult amusements in mind, I tried to picture the old set, and I could not. Activities like badminton were never even suggested by my parents when elders were on the premises. It seemed unfair to them. Their somewhat slower modes of moving did not strike me as sufficient cause to give up all sports and even dancing

My reasoning reverted to the likelihood that those in their sixties and above simply believed it was unseemly to do things that they were no longer expert at; that they would be committing a faux pas shocking to their offspring, and perhaps worrisome, too, due to a chance of injury.

My rebellion against this idea, this limitation, must have percolated in the farthest recesses of my brain. I don't recall "fixing" the rebellion as a major principle of my future, but it worked out that way regardless.

I liked certain sports, especially non-competitive ones, and never quit them. And this (the early 1960s) was well before the emergence of fitness as something like a national religion.

I continued to ice skate through my 20s, 30s, and 40s. I swam year round if indoor pools were nearby. I shed my frustrations (divorce, returning to the workforce fulltime after 18 years) by dancing wildly to hot music.

When I moved to a location without an ice rink, I bought the new-fangled option–rollerblades–and got the hang of them, using empty bank parking lots on Sundays in the small town where I lived.

The rollerblading continued when I moved back to Baltimore City, and, unwisely never bought the pads that are rightly recommended. One day at age 62, I tripped over a pebble in the street going about 20 miles per hour and landed on a knee. Though unbroken, it stayed swollen and bruised for weeks, and I decided that sport had to go. There were no rinks to make it safer.

In my 50s, near the end of my marriage, my ex-husband and I discovered kayaking. That relaxing fall and spring sport gave us most of any pleasure we then found together. I have my own boat now, but my current spouse is not keen on kayaking. It does take two people, at least at this age, to wrangle the boat onto a car roof.

Yes, I am very awkward getting into and out of the kayak. I am also slow climbing in and out of a swimming pool. And, it takes me 10 minutes or so to warm up while dancing. But would I give up these essential joys? Not a chance.

Anyone know another 70-ish woman who'd like to go paddling, for an hour or so per outing?

A LITTLE BEE WITH A BIG BUZZ

By: Joe Cullis

A little honeybee woke up in its bed. The rest of the hive was already all a-buzz. So the little bee stretched both its wings way way back then relaxed them again. Next it stretched out it legs two at a two at a two at a time till they were all stretched.

Then it crawled out of bed and it crawled through the hive. It knew the way well so to the entrance it scurried.

The little honeybee beat its wings real fast till away it did fly out into the morning bright sky. On this warm summer morning with few flowers in bloom the little bee had to fly quite far from home.

At last in the shade of a big tree it found a bright red flower. On a petal it landed and stuck in its head. It poked and it prodded but no nectar it found, so away it flew to search somewhere else.

The bright sun was hot. The little bee was about to give up when it saw a bright yellow flower glowing in sunlight. On a petal it landed then stuck in its head. The bee pulled up its head all drippy and wet! The nectar cup was full but not for much longer. The little bee drank and it drank till no more could fit in its little bee belly. The nectar was warm and sweet. So what's wrong with that?

The little honeybee crawled to the tip of a petal to sit and adjust to the weight of a full belly. As it sat the little bee's little head started to feel a little funny.

Now ready to fly it flapped its tiny wings. With buzz out of tune it rose at an angle and tilted far left. Instead of flying up and away to the hive with the nectar, it landed confused, on the ground.

The nectar in its belly sat too long in the flower and too long in the warm sun. The sugar turned into something more potent. This little honeybee now had a big big buzz.

The little honeybee with a big big buzz now sat confused. Which way to go, which way to the hive and how to get there?

So the little bee crawled to where it hoped home was. It crawled and it crawled and it crawled a while longer. Then the ground started tilting. The whole world was turning. The bee stopped crawling to see what was the matter. The bee's head felt so funny it took a long moment to figure it out.

The little bee with a big buzz was now up a tree trunk. It was in a tree drunk.

Maybe this was not so bad. Maybe higher up it could see where the hive is. So the little bee with a buzz crawled up and up up. Again the world started turning. The bee again stopped and again took a long moment to figure things out.

The little bee was out on a branch but on the down side. To the topside it crawled and here it saw a strange thing. It saw a big pile of sticks and leaves and feathers. Maybe from the top of this thing it could see the home hive.

The bee crawled stick to stick till it came to the top. Over the top it started down the other side when it heard a big noise and it saw a big thing. The things head was huge and it mouth even huger. Quick as it could the bee ran back over the sticks to the branch and back to the trunk. It crawled up higher away from the thing with the big head and the bigger mouth.

At the next branch the bee crawled out and out and onto a leaf. It sat on the leaf where the sun shone on it. Suddenly the leaf started to shake. A big long thing with too many legs was eating the leaf. The bee crawled as fast as it could away from the strange long thing and back to the trunk of the tree.

Maybe climbing the tree was not a good idea after all. But the big buzz in the little bee's head made it keep crawling higher and higher into the tree till it got to the very top.

At the very top of the tree the little bee with a big buzz could see a very long way. It saw the hive but was too tired to try to fly to it. Just then a bird swooped down and snatched up the bee in its sharp beak and flew away.

The little bee with the big buzz was no more.

POEMS

By: Nancy McCloy

Communion

The cupped trees held the sun for me.
As I, ascending to the highest heights
Stopped to drink at Life's all-consuming fire
And, as I drank, Fire took hold of me
Igniting all inborn seeds and stillness
Till grown and purified at last
World chaliced humanity was accepted by
The Father.

Quiet and Calm

Walking the Stations of the Cross
Outside the Cloister
Gardened in Tightly
by Wide Open Spaces
of Sky and Countryside
Surrounding Enclosures of Stone and Wood
Impermeable Protectors
Of Quiet and Calm

Sassy Sassafras

Too big for her britches
Shades of blue and green
Grey, brown, and foam white
Sizing up and down, in and out
Like the tide on a diet or a binge
How can all her travelers fit
So snuggly
As they preen about
From their afternoon idyll
On the Bay

High Tide on the Chester

High tide creeping, spilling into the street
Same as the birds, ducks, and geese
All colors and sizes
On this street, boasting of waterfront homes
and prices to pay
For a peek
Of the Chester.
Not necessary, if you visit the right time of
day

Along the Yough

I love trains
Especially their sounds
Mourning along the river rippling below
Mountain trails to visit on bikes and feet
High above
The river rippling below

Time

Timeless
All the time in the world
Lots of time
Timely
Time warp
Time sensitive
Half time
Make time For
Make time To
You can't
Stop time
Time out

For a Boy Immortal

Shock of black hair
Freckles sprinkled across the bridge of his nose
Stars dancing in his eyes
Easy, ornery and infectious grin

Persistence in all things
Half run always towards the objects of his desires
Mom, Dad, favorite teacher, whatever green
Us always trying to catch up to -

TO THERE

He's there already
Didn't take long
Spirit won over earth years
His job done

Our job
To catch up someday
With the boy immortal
David

SECOND THOUGHTS

By: Virginia Coleman

I was sitting on my suitcase in the crowded corridor of the train car. Each compartment was filled, as was the narrow aisle. Two German men, who reeked of alcohol, loomed over me talking in loud voices with much laughter.

We had left Luxembourg very early in the morning and the train had become more packed as we sped along the track from station to station. We still had a distance to travel before we reached Augsburg in the southern part of Germany where my husband was stationed with the U.S. Army.

A young woman who spoke English explained that many people were traveling due to a holiday. I learned during my time in Germany that rail was the primary mode of travel for both local commute and long distance travel. The rail system was convenient, speedy and modestly priced.

This was the mid 1950s when my boyfriend had learned he was being deployed to Germany for two years. So he proposed that we marry and I join him to start married life together in a foreign land. Since I was young, in love, and incredibly naïve the plan sounded wonderfully romantic.

My husband met my plane in Luxembourg where we spent two days sightseeing. Everyone seemed to speak English in the international city since we were staying at a large, old hotel and following the tourist trail. However English was less prevalent as we traveled through the German countryside.

My husband was a lowly Specialist Three and was not entitled to government housing so we would be living in German housing off the Army base. We became a part of the community of American couples living in Augsburg and surrounding villages. We considered ourselves the only ones truly experiencing real life in a foreign land as opposed to the people who lived on base in government housing. This could have been our way of dealing with being low man on the totem pole.

Now on our long ride through the German countryside when we were lucky enough to see through the train window, we saw vineyards on the hillsides above slow moving rivers and crumbling castles looming over the valley. I had spent the five months between our wedding and arriving in Luxembourg devouring guidebooks about Germany and German language phrase books. The Germany I pictured was somewhere between a Mario Lanza operetta and Heidi in the Alps with sweet little goats wearing bells. The picturesque countryside only increased my excitement at the thought of living in these storybook surroundings for the next twenty months.

We arrived in Augsburg about 4 a.m. and sat in the train station until the American Express Office opened so I could change my money to marks. Lack of good planning marked a slow start to our first day in Augsburg. The core of the city is enclosed by its old medieval wall and surrounded by dwellings from the many years since, fanned out in layers. The rebuilding from World War II was taking place during our time there and the city was reaching into the countryside. In a short period of time it seemed we were traveling through time from the inner city to the army base near the edge of town.

The exhilaration I had felt for the past five days was rapidly giving way to exhausting fatigue. By late afternoon we had taken care of military procedure and could finally climb into a taxi to take us to a small gasthaus in a nearby village where we would stay until our apartment, in that same village, would become available. Rain was pouring down in torrents as we proceeded down a muddy, rut filled road toward the gasthaus which combined the services of bar, restaurant and rooming house for the small town.

As we entered the front door, music and laughter filled the air along with smell of roasting meat, beer and cigarette smoke. A wedding reception was being held in every available space in the building. The bride, dressed in white, stood by the door looking only slightly less awe stricken than I felt. Climbing the stairs to our room we found that a game resembling shuffleboard had been set up in the corridor and it had attracted a good crowd of young men.

We shut the door of our room as I looked around. It was small by any standard with little furniture, linoleum on the floor and a naked light bulb hanging from the ceiling fixture. I was faced with a very drab basic room drenched with the thud of the shuffleboard and laughter coming through the wall. However it contained an Honest-to-God bed, which I fell into gratefully.

The next morning my husband left early to go to the base while I slept. When I awoke in the middle of the morning, the room was dark and dreary. I walked to the window where rain slid down the glass. I stood with my head against the window looking out at the backyard flooded with muddy, brown water. Gloomy weather, gloomy room, gloomy me! I hadn't seen this page in my glowing guidebook to Germany.

ANGEL MOON

By: Ronny Aseltine

She sat there trying to "Be still" as her father, in a stern tone, had instructed her. He was now busy chatting with the strangers seated to his left and she was sitting there staring at her red Mary-Janes trying not to move. The seat in the movie theatre was uncomfortable because if she sat back in the seat, the scratchy front edge of the seat was at her calves, and her feet stuck out in front of her. She had thought about crossing her legs and sitting Indian style but her father had told her that young ladies were not to sit like that in a public. So, she sat and stared at her red shoes. She liked them and wondered why her mother had wanted her to wear the black shoes instead.

The night before, Cricket had taken an old newspaper and placed it under the shoes before she carefully polished them, just as her father had instructed her, along with her older brother and sister, a few months earlier. When she woke up from her nap in that afternoon, she put on her slip and her pink dress with ruffles at the hem. Her mother had taken them out of the closet for her after lunch. She put on her socks and shoes. Cricket then went to her mother for help with the buttons at the back of the dress.

First her mother had been busy with the baby and then she had to go get something off the stove. Cricket trailed along silently behind her mother as she took the baby's bottles out of the big pot on the stove and set them on a tea towel to dry. Then her mother started peeling potatoes to put in another pot and when she finished she took the meat loaf out of the refrigerator and put it in the oven. The baby began crying again and Cricket followed her mother toward the crib but her mother turned and said with her impatient voice,

"You will just have to wait until I get to you, the whole world does not revolve around you, you know. Go and change your shoes. Never wear red with pink," said her mother.

Cricket thought about the whole world revolving. The world is so gigantic and she felt so small, even for a girl who was turning six years old today. The idea of something that big revolving around her made her anxious, the way she had felt when the family had gone to the Delaware Water Gap. It had been her first look at real mountains. Her father had parked the car where they could look up at all the mountains surrounding them.

It seemed imposing to a little girl who was used to the flat lands of southern New Jersey. She'd felt like a cheerio lying in the bottom of a bowl, about to be swallowed or flooded.

Cricket went and stood in the doorway to her older brother's room and stared at the globe on his desk. That is the world, she thought. She remembered a project her sister had done for school. Zann had made spheres out of Paper Mache to represent all of the planets. She'd painted them different colors and then hung them with strings from a straightened wire coat hanger. Her sister had told her that the earth was a planet and that all the planets revolved around the sun and that the sun was a huge ball of fire and hotter than the kitchen stove.

If the world revolved around her she would have to get near the sun and that was impossible. She couldn't get anywhere unless she was driven there or if she rode her sister's bike. She knew that she couldn't get to the sun. Cricket liked the sun. When it was out, it brought the daylight and that was good because she was afraid of the dark. But at night when she was in her bed sometimes she could see the moon from her window and that always made her feel like a light inside her had been lit.

Sometimes she would stay awake to watch it in the dark sky. She believed that the angels lived inside the moon and they made the light for the moon with their love. She believed the angels sent love to people needing love and that they could make people safe, even in the dark. She loved the moon even though she was afraid of the dark that came with it.

Just then her brother came into his room from the hall, "Get out of my room stupid," he said, slapping her head as he passed her in the doorway. She felt like crying but she did not want anyone to know she felt hurt. She did not want to feel sad

Cricket went to her room and waited for her mother. It began to feel like she probably wouldn't have time. After a while she took off her dress and buttoned all the buttons on her dress and tried to put it on again but it would not go over her head. So she unbuttoned the top button and tried again. It went over her head this time. She retied her sash and twisted it around so that the bow would be in the back. She did not change her shoes. She was ready to go.

She decided to stay on her bed until it was time to leave. She would look at books and maybe no one would yell at her. After a while her brother called out, "Hey dummy! It's time to go see your dumb movie, get out of here."

Cricket went to wait by the front door. Presently her father came into the hall, glanced at her and reached for his hat from the hallstand. As he opened the door, her mother came rushing toward them. "Oh, you haven't eaten anything, you can't go yet!"

"Well then we aren't going." Her father replied. "It's twenty minutes to six. If we don't go now, we won't go."

Cricket's heart sank; the movie was her big birthday present. Cricket was the only girl in the first grade who hadn't seen Snow White and the Seven Dwarfs. She looked hopefully up into her mothers face.

"Oh well, it's not ready yet, I guess you can eat when you get back." her mother relented.

"I didn't get out of that lunch until three," said her father, "so that will work for me. Let's go."

Now the movie was going to start, the previews were coming. She could not see very well because she was too small to see over the seat in front of her but she was glad because the previews showed some scary people shooting and yelling at each other. Then there was a cartoon. She didn't really enjoy that either. She didn't think a rabbit being chased by a man with a gun was funny. It was too close to her nightmares.

She glanced over at the people to her father's left. The man was sitting with his daughter on his lap, she leaning back into his chest and sucking her thumb. Her own father was staring straight ahead. He was there but he never spoke to her and rarely looked at her. She was all right with this because if he didn't speak, he didn't yell and he didn't hit.

When Snow White began she wanted to see around the person in front of her so she edged up on the arm of the seat on her right, trying to gain some height. The girl sitting to her right was a big girl, maybe ten or eleven. " Can't you see? Here," the girl whispered, "take my coat and sit on it." Cricket stared at her with big eyes. "Go on take it and sit on it." The big girl had bundled her coat and was trying to tuck the bundled coat under Cricket. "Thank you" said Cricket shyly as she repositioned herself on the coat and leaned further into the right side of her seat.

When the frightening part came with the witch and the poison apple, Cricket put her head down; the girl reached over and took her hand. At one point her father looked at them and said in a stern voice, "What are you doing?" but the big girl looked at him squarely and said: "It's the scary part, you are supposed to hold hands." Her father said nothing and looked straight ahead.

When the movie was over Cricket got up and gave the big girl her coat. "Did you like the movie?" asked the big girl.

"Oh yes" answered Cricket.

"Me too," said the big girl. "I've seen it three times now. Bye-bye."

Cricket felt very shy but she waved and smiled watching the girl put on her now-wrinkled coat, as she got ready to leave.

The big girl's mother put her arm around the girl's shoulder as they walked away. Cricket's father was talking to the man next to him again. The man was putting a coat on the little girl who was now leaning sleepily against him.

Cricket's father looked down at her, put his hat on his head and said: "Let's go." He started up the aisle ahead of her and went through the door. She had not even thought about bringing a coat and it had become a chilly September evening.

Cricket hurried behind her father trying to keep up with him. When they got away from the crowd and the streetlights and into the darkened parking lot, Cricket became aware of the white-blue light shining down from high above. Her heart lifted as she looked up at the big full moon, *Oh*! She thought. *The angels are here for my birthday and they are sending their love.*

And all the way home, along the rural roads, she watched the moon and felt the cover of angel light surrounding her.

POEMS

By: Amethyst McNabb

One on the Earth

In the wake of modernity
We have lost
Our connection
To the indigenous Eden
Of Gaia's mantle

We have forgotten
To embrace
Our ancestors
We have overlooked
Our original Oneness

Compassion is priceless
Benevolence divine
Can we spare one minute
In our hurried lives
To extend a loving word, deed
Or intention?

Solstice Bride

Today I am Aphrodite, Astarte, Psyche, Rhiannon
The archetype of every bride since the dawn of time
The lover, the loved
The sun at its zenith enriches my body and soul
In my frosty satin I am the moon, pale and luminous
My milky veil levitates around me
A participant in this sacred dance
As a dozen drumming hands carry my naked feet
joyously forward
To a promise of lifetime love
Inscribing the first page in the story of our marriage

Everything I Need

I have returned to my true Home
My true Self
In this place the elements embrace
Sand, Sea, Sun, Sky
Seagulls and Spirit soaring

Three dawns, a thousand miles
A lifetime ago
An incomplete woman, a colorless life
Monotony mirroring winter's barren landscape
Abandoned and dying, months from rebirth

The southbound highway-the 18 hour cure
The pewter clouds are rolled away
Revealing a new stage
Painted with aqua, magenta, and jungle green
The shades of Life, and amplified Joy
A masterpiece by the Creator

As my skin returns to caramel
Obligations fall away
Like footprints claimed by the surf
Erasing any trace of my existence
I am empty
I have everything I need

Haikus for Mindfulness

Bonfire magic
Watching sparks crackle against
Starlit mountain sky

Connected culture
An obstacle on the path
Of simpler lifestyle

1000 channels
Of mostly mindless drivel
I'd rather watch squirrels

A path through the reeds
With blue and green dragonflies
The Zen of the marsh

Summer storm yoga
Breathing in the lightning
Breathing out-thunder

Time is relative
Mindfulness of the present
Can stretch each moment

Photographs are no
Substitute for presence so
Live deeply instead

Night Meditation

The sounds of the night
The raspy mating call of frogs
The whistle of birds
The neighbor's pool filling
That sounds like gentle rain
The kamikaze stinkbugs
Around my porch light
A critter scurrying through the leaves
A quiet mind

Walking the Dog at Dawn

Morning sun and light drizzle
Simultaneously kiss my hair
And rustle the pines, oaks and sassafras
While a pair of periwinkle butterflies
Glide in an aerial waltz

Dumb Animals?

Some people call our
Furred and feathered friends "stupid"
I do not agree

Squirrels do not hurry
But they still manage to store
Acorns for winter

Birds fly leisurely
While they navigate thousand
Mile flights to the south

Leopards hunt only
What they need to feed their cubs
Then sleep in the sun

We rush constantly
To accomplish more each day
Like treadmill hamsters

God Beyond Boundaries

Is the prayer discounted
If it's not Saturday, Sunday, Christmas, or Solstice
Or if you neglect to kneel, bow, or sit in lotus pose?

Is the ritual invalid
Without a cross, prayer rug, candles, or incense
Or if you forget the words, or transpose the
elements?

Does God ignore
If you call him by another cultures' name
Or somewhere besides a church, temple, or mosque?

Is God defined by gender or nationality?
And if you don't match the superficial description
Are you "unchosen," flawed, doomed to an
unfortunate afterlife?

Is God limited to exist
In the words of our ancestors?
In the cycles of the harvest? Or beyond the stars?

NO!

I will not "like" you
Or "friend" you
Or "re-tweet" your ad

I will not "follow"
Or "pin" you
It's all just a fad

I don't want your flyer
Your freebies
Or your dumb plastic bag

I don't need your coupons
I don't need your app
And don't you dare call me
When I'm taking my nap

So keep your "rewards points"
Your credit cards too
And I'll pay with cash
Like sane people do

The Season's upon us
Oh Lord what a shame
That Christ doesn't love me
If I don't spend in his name!

A NIGHT IN THE COUNTRY

By: Frances Reed

Darkness came quickly, moving from the soft glow of twilight to night's sooty blackness.

It startled Olivia as to how dark it was. In the city it was never totally dark. There was always an orange tint to the sky that lit the world like a nightlight. Not brightly, but with a friendly softness. Night in the country, she was discovering, was completely different. Pressing forward like a threat, and definitely *non*-friendly. Shadows here were deeper and tugged at her imagination in ways they never did in the city. Olivia was sure there must be wild animals, or worse, wilder men, lurking in the darkness. Waiting for her.

The old house rattled and creaked as she made her way up the three story hanging staircase, her hand gripping the handrail, worn silken smooth from generations of hands sliding over its surface. The sharp, ugly bare hall light bulb casting her flickering shadow on the wall as she climbed. Shivering, when the house made noises she wasn't used to, Olivia hurried along the corridor towards the room she'd chosen earlier, uncomfortably aware of the sudden leaping of her heart, spooked further by the old windows, clattering in the wind that sprang up as night fell.

Olivia was now wishing she'd waited until morning to arrive. Somehow big old houses were friendlier during daytime. She hadn't thought about being alone when she arrived, late in the afternoon. Then, with the western sun gilding the house, and the golden glow softening the peeling paint, she'd felt welcomed, and happy to finally be here.

She'd explored the house again. Finding two rooms not seen before. Olivia had been sure that she'd been in all the rooms when she was there previously. But what did two more rooms matter when there were so many? Twenty, no, twenty-two rooms. All that space and all that work. The old 1880s summer hotel had been a true find and she was eager to start its renovation, but the first thing she needed was a bedroom.

The room Olivia selected to sleep in was in the front of the house on the second level. She had chosen this bedroom because of its triple bay windows facing east. The windows were tall elegant Victorian sash windows running from about two feet above the floor almost to the ceiling. The bed was placed with it's back to the middle window, and was flanked on either side by the other two windows. Her choice made. Olivia opened the windows to air out the room, and made up the bed.

Now, she was almost running to that room, her shadow chasing gamely after her. She reached the bedroom, throwing herself through the door, slamming it shut behind her, fear twisting her insides, for no real reason other than the unexpected terror of being on her own, at night, and in a house with twenty-two rooms that could hold *anything*. Not only alone, but also way out in the country in a house with no locks. Worse, with no close neighbors, just open farmland between her and the next nearest house.

Breathing fast, feeling foolish, but still afraid, Olivia moved to the bed and switched on the bedside lamp. Then turned back to the door to secure it with a chair wedged under the doorknob. She closed two of the windows, hesitating over the third but finally leaving it cracked open. She needed the fresh air.

Feeling immeasurably better, now she was safely cocooned in a room, closed off from the rest of the newly scary house, Olivia went to bed. Forcing herself to focus on decorating, she drifted off to sleep, her fears easing away, as she occupied her mind with plans for improvements.

Initially she wasn't sure what woke her, but *something* startled her awake, her heart once again accelerating, fear crowding in on her. She lay listening, but the house was quiet, the wind that rattled the windows earlier was gone. Moonlight trickled across the floor from a fourth window and onto the chair still firmly wedged under the bedroom door. A quick glance at her watch told her it was barely past 3am. Snuggling back under the covers, thinking it must have been a bad dream that woke her, Olivia was sliding into sleep again when she heard the noise…in her almost asleep state she was idly wondering what it was when she realized it was… heavy breathing, and it was in the room *with* her.

It was at that point that every night terror that she had ever experienced swamped her. Bile rose in her throat as she realized she'd locked herself in the bedroom with no means of escape, and in a room at least sixteen feet off the ground, and with no ladder. Olivia lay very still, listening to the breathing sounds. In, Out, In, Out– almost asthmatic in sound. In, Out. In. Out. For almost five minutes she lay trembling, waiting with all the worst possible scenarios flooding her mind.

It was then that Olivia realized: The breathing wasn't coming from *inside* the room; it was coming in through the open window. The man, for she was sure it was a man, must be standing outside on the porch roof, waiting to make sure she was asleep before making his move.

Instantly Olivia knew what to do. Throwing off the covers she dived for the open window screaming:

"Whoever you are, I have a gun! If you come in here I'll shoot! Go away! I've called the police – they are on their way. Leave! Go!"

She slammed the window closed, locked it, and waited.

Nothing.

And waited.

Nothing.

After half an hour, she crawled back into bed and slept fitfully until the sun rose pouring its light through the three windows, waking her.

Everything looked different in the morning; Olivia was happy and grateful to be alive. She danced downstairs, resisting the temptation to slide down the bannister, made herself a cup of coffee and went outside, walking to the front of the house to see if she could find out how the man had climbed up to outside her window.

Olivia was standing outside looking upwards when she heard the sound again: Heavy breathing, coming from just behind her. She froze.

In. Out.

In. Out.

Turning around, very slowly, Olivia's hazel eyes locked eyes with the dark brown ones of the source of all her terror. Seconds later she was helpless with laughter.

She'd never known a cow could breathe so loudly.

PUKE

By: Larry Samuels

Ben Spooner, a 2nd Class Petty Officer, the rate of Sergeant, watched as the sweat rolled down the mottled, plump face of Fireman Apprentice Allen Pute. He looked like a glistening wet statue as he stood there in his dripping, rumpled dungaree uniform, staring through the peephole at the 3000° F flames roaring in the one-story high firebox of 1A boiler. His appearance matched the nickname that was bestowed on him soon after he had reported to the boiler room on this U.S. Navy destroyer – "Puke."

Nicknames were prevalent among the crew, with the most common ones shortening last names, or otherwise highlighting some feature of one's physical presence or personality. Ben had invariably acquired the handle "Gentle Ben," however; the men didn't call him that to his face. Ben was a twenty-five year old, 5'8" tall block of a man, with blonde hair cut to standard military length, clean-shaven, with a square face containing dark blue eyes. He did not look at all gentle, although he was fair and helpful to his men.

Allen, a squat nineteen-year old with short fuzzy brown hair and pin-set brown eyes, had his nickname culled from Pute, but not altogether derived from the sound or spelling. He had earned it because of his attitude and performance. The dull expression on his face seemed to indicate little ambition or interest.

Ben thought about Allen's first day in the fire room three months before, when he descended the almost vertical fifteen-foot ladder, backwards. A sailor was supposed to walk down a ladder facing forward, so that one could see what was below, and to balance oneself in pitching seas. On this first day, though, in port, the ship was not moving and the boilers were not firing.

"Allen Pute, Fireman Apprentice, reporting," he had said to no one in particular.

"I know your name," Frank "Beef" Johnson, the large-framed 1st Class Petty Officer answered him irritably. "We were all on the fantail this morning for muster, don't you remember?"

"I was just saying what I thought you were supposed to say," he mumbled.

"Don't you be thinking now, Pute, get you in trouble," Tommy Grant, one of the 3rd Class Petty Officers said jokingly.

Some of the others, Dominick "Bull," Anton, Ted "Wheels" Singleton, and Drayton "House" Houser, laughed. That should have been the moment for Allen to join in the humor, to say something friendly, but he just stood there. The crew in this fire room was a tight, exclusive group, very judgmental and they formed their opinions of new members almost immediately. A new man had to prove himself quickly. Allen had not made much of an impression.

That first day of Allen's arrival, Brad Sorenson, one of the supervising 3rd Class Petty Officers, handed out work assignments. "All right everyone, listen up. Joey and 'Steely', we need the oil changed in #2 air compressor. 'Peaches', Smitty, take the booster pump coupling replacement."

As he finished assigning work, Allen stood there uncertainly. Some new men might have taken the initiative and asked Brad what they should do, since he hadn't been given a specific task.

Ben had seen other new men face up to being in a new situation, and others to not handle it very well. He wanted to give Allen the benefit that he was just shy and might come around. Unfortunately, Allen's next reaction dashed this hope.

Brad said evenly, "Pute, I want you to get a set of gloves from that locker over there, a paint scraper and a bucket. Go to the corner near that fuel pump and lift up a deck plate, then crawl in, make yourself comfortable and start cleaning out the muck in that section of the bilges. You can come up for air in about an hour to grab a smoke, so let's get started."

Allen had looked blankly at Brad. He was supposed to have known, as everyone else in the Navy knew, that all new sailors assigned to the engineering spaces started out by cleaning the bilges. Once the steam plant was operational and they were at sea, Allen would be trained to make regularly scheduled rounds of the system, recording machinery temperature and pressure readings. For now, while at cold iron, he would have to spend time with his nose to the keel of the ship.

Allen didn't move. He said petulantly, "I don't really want to do that. I've got on clean dungarees. Why don't you give me something else to do?"

Brad and Ben had looked at each other, surprise mirrored on their faces. Non-rated Firemen Apprentices did not say these things to Petty Officers. Several of the crew still standing there waited for the hammer to fall.

"Listen up, Pute," Brad continued evenly, but with an edge. "You get yourself out of my face, grab your gear and put your fat little body into those bilges now, or you will remain there for the rest of your enlistment. Do you understand what I'm saying?"

Allen's pink, mushy face had lost a bit of its color. No one else moved. "OK," he said, "But I'm not going to like it."

"Look, snipe," Brad hissed, "I don't care. This isn't your first day in the Navy. You're going to do what you're told when you're told. If you behave yourself while attached to this gang you may improve your lot in life."

Ben had piped in, "Listen to what he's saying. Everyone pulls their own weight down here, and we're a team. I thought you had this figured out from Boot Camp."

Brad said, "You know sailor, from now on, we're going to call you "Puke," until you can be worthy of getting your name back. That's all bud, now get going."

Puke's little eyes had widened and his back went stiff. Now he looked like a frightened pumpkin. He turned and walked toward the tool locker. Ben had thought that Allen deserved his new name, for not having the sense to bond with this group. He had felt uneasy, however, about having to rely on a guy like Puke in the ensuing period when they would be at sea in their combat role.

Brad said, "Hey, we better keep an eye on this guy."

"I'm hoping we can change his attitude as we go along," answered Ben.

"I don't know, I think it'll just get worse. He's not our kind of people."

"We have to hope," Ben countered. "I'm not going to ride him too hard while we're in port; maybe that will help."

"All right, I'll stay out of the way for awhile, too."

"OK, let's see if I can help him see the light."

During the next two weeks, even though Ben made the effort to include Allen, Puke did not respond very well. At sea, he would either continue to fail in adversity or he would recover when faced with the chance to prove himself. Ben would just have to wait.

Now that they were at sea, with the plant at full steam, it was deafening in the fire room. Here, below the waterline just beyond the hull, and a few feet above the murky depths of this Navy destroyer, steam was produced for the main engines, generators and auxiliaries. They were on Yankee Station in the Gulf of Tonkin, 20,000 yards off the coast of Vietnam in 1972, during the waning days of the war.

At 110° F, the temperature on the lower level was at least 30° F cooler than on the upper level, which contained other essential equipment. This was cooler still, though, than the 180° F temperature on top of the boilers, where some of the men were scraping paint at this very moment. Their only relief from the heat were huge "elephant trunks" blowing air directly on them, tapped from the topside fresh air intake fans.

The fire room crew was made up of sailors of a range of technical abilities, who faced their environment with varying degrees of acceptance and complaint. They were enlisted men, almost property, but skilled. It was almost inconceivable that humans could work in these

61

conditions, but they did, eating a finger full of salt tablets while the blood in their veins seemed to thin out to the viscosity of hot motor oil running through a race car engine.

During one of his two daily four-hour watches, Ben turned the corner at 1A boiler and immediately saw a steaming stream of water shooting out from the automatic valve, which controlled the speed and capacity of the pump used for fighting fires.

This repair could not wait. The pump was critical to safety and operational readiness. The ship was responsible for picking up fighter pilots who might crash into the sea following raids on shore targets from the aircraft carrier that the destroyer was assigned to on this day and the ability to fight any onboard fires was not debatable.

This was also imperative while providing gunfire support for South Vietnamese troop operations on other days, just south of Quang Tri City, near the demilitarized zone. Sometimes the Viet Cong would shoot back at them. The ship had been hit with shrapnel on two occasions this past fifty-four days underway. During these operations, the crew would be at their workstations and standing watches–normal routine.

Sometimes, however, the entire ship's crew would be at General Quarters, or Battle Stations, when radar picked up an unidentified contact that could be a potential enemy aircraft or missile. In all cases, this fire pump needed to function properly in order to fight a shipboard fire. Since this was on Ben's watch, he would be accountable for implementing corrective action.

He walked across the deck plates and said to Frank, the senior supervisor, "Looks like the diaphragm and gasket in the fire pump governor are shot. Without full power, we don't have enough water pressure."

Beef picked up the 5J circuit phone and called the forward engine room, explaining conditions. The Chief Engineer, Lieutenant Andrew Hardin, climbed down the two ladders to the lower level.

"Beef, Ben, what's it going to take to get this under control?" he asked them. He respected his Petty Officers for their knowledge of the plant.

"Sir, if we can just isolate that pump for maybe about two hours, Ben here can make the repair," Beef said.

Ben said, "We can fix this. I've done this one before, though not under these circumstances while plane guarding."

"Alright," agreed Lt. Hardin, "I'll inform the Bridge."

Frank said to Ben, "Who do you want to work with?"

Ben thought about his usual workers, always dependable. Ben considered that either Tommy, or Dominick, or anyone of the boiler gang knew what they were doing technically. He was confident that each one of them would be fine for this repair.

Then he thought about Puke. He was just now working in the overhead above the exhaust steam condenser on the upper level, scraping and painting the angle iron supports. Unfortunately, he had not improved as much as Ben had hoped he would. For example, while underway, Ben had been told by one of the non-rated men of the need to sometimes have to wake Allen a second time from sleep, since he didn't spring into action to relieve the watch. This was unacceptable–every watch stander was entitled to be relieved at fifteen minutes before the hour of their four-hour watch.

His nickname continued to fit, not only mimicking his real name, but from his persistent personal shortcomings and poor behavior. As a senior Petty Officer, Ben felt responsible for bringing Allen into the fold by treating him with respect and including him on repair operations, as part of his training.

Even today, while most of the other crew didn't like what they were assigned to, they might have grumbled amongst themselves, but they didn't complain to their supervisor. Puke had whined straight back about working in the heat, just as he had complained when he first arrived on board. It didn't make any difference. The work had to get done, and these boiler room sailors had to do it.

Ben was willing to have Puke redeem himself. He could have chosen any one of his men, instead, he answered Frank, "I'll take Puke."

"OK, have one of the guys call Puke to come below, we've got a job for him."

Puke extricated himself from the engulfing tangle of steel and presented himself to Ben and Beef.

"Allen, the fire pump needs a diaphragm. I want you to learn something new and to have a hand in something important. You know we have to be ready immediately to wash down any fuel spill or put out a fire while we're chasing this carrier. You up for that?" Ben asked him.

Allen said, "Wow, that sure beats scraping paint."

"OK, then, what do you think we'll need, and what's a diaphragm?" Ben asked him.

Puke hesitated. "We'll need wrenches to fit, a hammer, new gasket material, a scraper and a drift pin. The diaphragm? It's a steel disc to hold the steam supply pressure and spring tension to control the pump speed. That's right?"

"That's good, Allen. Let's go."

Ben said, "Go ahead and shut down the steam and sea water valves. The ship is now without fire main service on the port side."

Puke said, "We have to work fast. We could need that pump anytime."

"Good thinking, buddy," said Ben.

They hammered the flange nuts loose, Puke holding the wrenches. They removed the valve onto the deck plates, dismantled the valve and Puke set the new diaphragm in place.

"Let me make the gasket," Allen said.

"Go right ahead."

They lifted the valve in place and Puke tightened the bolts. Ben said, "That's good, you tightened them in sequence."

"Sure, I did think of that."

Ben asked, "OK, what would you do next?"

"I'd open the suction and discharge, and cut in cooling water to the shaft packing glands."

"You're thinking sharp here," said Ben.

They tested for leaks by cracking open the exhaust valve, then letting in 600 pounds per square inch of 500° F steam.

"Everything looks good to me," said Ben. "Let's bring the discharge pressure up. You adjust the spring. Watch your gauge."

Puke used a large screwdriver to adjust it until the pump was up to speed. Although it had been a fairly straightforward repair, it was potentially dangerous under emergency conditions.

As they were cleaning up, Ben asked, "What did you do before the Navy?"

"Well, I'm from a small town in Pennsylvania, where I graduated from high school. I didn't do much except help my dad plant soybeans. I didn't have a chance to go anywhere, so I joined up, but I didn't really want to, I just didn't want to get drafted into the Army. I'm really glad you let me work with you, Ben. No one likes to work with me since I sometimes don't get things right."

"Well, you did OK for me. Good job."

They walked across the deck plates to Frank. "Pump tested and on the line," Ben reported. Frank contacted Main Control and Lt. Hardin gave Puke and Ben the customary, ubiquitous Navy accolade, "Well done!"

It can't be said that the rest of Puke's time in the fire room was totally less than stellar, however, the triumph today was hoped by Ben to be a positive turning point in Allen's personal and professional development.

Ben put this method into practice in various situations later in his service. Just a little mentoring and positive reinforcement can go a long way to helping someone improve themselves. Ben thought about what was more important than their success was the look on the face of Allen when they finished. Through the sweat and the grime, Puke was smiling.

THE INHERITANCE

By: Peggy Jaegly

"Fay! FAY! I need more water!" The shouted summons was accompanied by the incessant ringing of a bell.

Fayola sighed. She replaced the case inside the safe without having time to open it. She gently shut the door to the wall vault. She had discovered its hiding place behind the painting when dusting. "Coming!" she answered with feigned cheerfulness.

For what seemed like the umpteenth time that day, she lumbered over to the stairs and slowly hefted her large body, grunting with each step. It was only 10 a.m. Two years ago, Fay offered to move into this mansion to take care of her bedridden cousin. With the collapse of the economy, she had had to short sell her own modest home and was still paying off the debt caused by the shortfall. Without Gertrude falling ill and the opportunity it presented, she would have been homeless.

At first, everyone thought she was an angel, to sacrifice her own independence to take care of a 98-year-old relative. She didn't let them know the true reason. But now that she was here, she intended to remain the mistress of this lovely home. She deserved it. Gertrude, though bedridden, proved to be more stout and headstrong than Fay realized. Her cousin's demands were endless. She couldn't believe the old woman hadn't kicked the bucket yet.

"Fay, are you coming?" Another shout emitted from Gertrude's bedroom.

"I sure am," Fay called back. She placed a hand on her lower back to ease its pain. *If I can help it, this will be the last time.* She climbed the last two steps with a new determination.

A week later, Fayola, dressed in black, lowered herself into the most comfortable chair, certain of success. A gaggle of infrequent visiting relatives, with unsettled anticipation, milled about the large parlor of the Victorian house she expected would be hers in a few minutes. *Vultures hovering for the spoils*, thought Fay. *Where had they been for the last two and half years while I slaved taking care of Gertrude?*

Two elderly women entered the room and momentarily Fayola froze with anxiety. Her cousin's sisters! She recognized them from their photos, which Gertrude had framed, in her living room. Bea and Elsie. Fayola forced herself to take a deep breath. She reached into her purse for a handkerchief and dabbed at her eyes. She wanted them to see how upset she was at Gertrude's passing.

They lived in another state. Fayola had discouraged them from visiting where she had been residing in Gertrude's house in Chestertown. Fay loved living in this exclusive neighborhood on the Chester River. The million-dollar plus home had a temperature controlled wine room, a gourmet kitchen, and a lovely master suite with a sitting room. Fay wanted to keep this luxury for herself. She certainly deserved it.

Fay always pretended that she was glad Gertrude's sisters called and also pretended that she hated telling them that Gertrude's health precluded them visiting. When they insisted on visiting, Fayola would slip a Valium to Gertrude so she slept most of the time, when they or any other relative or friend ventured inside the house.

Bea and Elsie sent cards, but Fayola easily intercepted them when she retrieved the mail for the bed bound Gertrude. The shredder had been busy. Gertrude had many friends, but Fayola made certain her cousin knew that it was her and her alone, who really cared for her.

If Gertrude ever got to the phone before she did, Fayola would explain later to Bea and Elsie about Gertrude's growing dementia. Of course, that's why she didn't remember receiving their notes. They didn't ever offer any monetary support for their sister or to her, for that matter. Didn't the whole family know Gertrude was a rich widow? When Gertrude's husband was alive, they had spent much of their adult lives on an endless vacation, jetting all over the world. *What was she worried about?* She knew who would inherit everything. It was going to be the person who deserved it the most, after all her years of *loving and selfless* service... herself. In fact, she could be magnanimous. She popped up from her chair.

"Bea! Elsie! I'd recognize you in an instant from the photo albums that Gertrude and I would spend such lovely times looking at. Oh, I'm so sorry that we have to meet, after all this time, under these circumstances. I just can't believe..." Fayola wiped her dry eyes, "that she's gone. Oh, here, please take this seat, Bea. I'll find a chair for you, Elsie."

"Um, well, thank you, Fay," Bea responded tonelessly. Elsie smiled with tense lips and averted her eyes downward.

Hmpf. Why were they being so cold? Oh well, what did she have to worry about? Hadn't her cousin promised her that she would be remembered in her will? Hadn't Fayola sacrificed her personal life, except for occasional jaunts to Atlantic City, to take care of her? Her cousin had been bed bound, hooked up to tubes and body bags. They were stinky jobs to empty and clean every day. Once a week, she had to clean her patient's Foley catheter. Gertrude was often cranky and always demanding. Three times a day, Fayola had patiently smiled while she fed her meals. She changed her sheets when her cousin got sick or the bags leaked. She wiped up vomit from the floors. She made sure she took her oxygen treatments. She did loads and loads of laundry. And her back, her aching back. Gertrude's hefty frame had worn out her spine, as she moved her from bed to wheelchair and back again. All the while, she never let on how distasteful it all was. As far as Gertrude was concerned, she was her angel, best friend and savior all rolled into one. Fayola did it all for the payoff. She deserved every penny, or the thousands of dollars, she'd be receiving. *Damn the relatives!*

Oh sure, she'd taken a bauble here and there to sell. She'd learned how to hawk items without ever leaving the house, using a computer she'd borrowed. She wasn't really all that savvy with the technology, but she'd played around with it enough to discover a couple of lists on the Internet that were, to her, like a worldwide garage sale. Those proceeds paid for her wild nights at the blackjack tables. But a streak of losses had left creditors pressing her for payment. Fayola devised the perfect plan. A plump pillow pressed down on her cousin's face, instead of underneath her head accelerated today's reading of the will. Finally, she'd get what she deserved. No one questioned a 98-year-old, sick woman dying. No one suspected foul play.

The attorney strode in with Mr. Smartee Pants, her cousin's beloved cat, padding behind him. *That damn cat! Gertrude loved that cat as if it were her flesh and blood. What did that snooty cat ever do to help?* Fayola had to resume her allergy medicine to control her adverse reaction to that fat fur ball. After everyone left today, that'd be first on her to do list – a visit to the animal pound.

The lawyer seated himself behind the grand oak desk and shifted some papers. Mr. Smartee Pants jumped onto the window seat and curled up in the sunlight. Fayola's wandering thoughts blotted out his first words, but she focused now as he read, trying to hide the wide grin that fought to burst across her face.

"Being of sound mind and body…" the attorney droned, "…the balance of my estate including the house, the outbuildings and land, I bequeath to my constant, trusted companion…"

Fayola smiled and sat straighter. She'd been the only one around the old woman. It could only be her.

"…Mr. Smartee Pants," the lawyer read.

Fayola heard a collective gasp in the room, including her own. She held her breath as the lawyer continued.

"…and for her devotion and length of service and because I realize more than anyone, the deeds for which she should be rewarded, I bequeath to my cousin, Fayola Martin, my collection of five gold Amazonian coins."

"Those are worth almost two million," grumbled a relative.

Sweat beaded on Fayola's forehead. *They had been worth two million?* Her stomach churned like laundry in an overloaded washer. *How had her cousin known what she'd done?*

Over time, she had sold each gold coin for a couple hundred bucks apiece and replaced it with a fake. It wasn't like her cousin could get out of bed to check. Now they belonged to her.

Mr. Smartee Pants meowed and brushed around her ankles on his way out.

NADIA

By: Nancy Hartman

I can recall the brief meeting as clearly as if it had happened last night. It was the Monday before Thanksgiving, a moonless evening sketched with traces of softly falling snow.

Some of us had second thoughts about going. Diane was concerned about the snowy forecast for the evening. Gretchen said she was having a rough day at the office, and Elaine said that the parents probably wouldn't even notice we were there. I'm sure that none of us had wanted to go to a funeral parlor.

We had come to pay our "respects," as they say, to Nadia and her parents. The news had become official in the obituary section of the Monday morning newspaper. Nadia Koori had died Sunday morning at the age of 26. She left behind her parents, an older sister, and a brother-in-law. Visiting hours would be from 7 to 9 on Monday evening at the Holton Funeral Parlor. She would be buried Wednesday in a private ceremony.

It was because of Lexy that we heard about the news so quickly. A member of our high school group, Lexy was the only person, to anyone's knowledge, who had kept in touch with Nadia after graduation.

On our way to the funeral home, Lexy had pointed out the building, only a framework of which had been constructed. The seven-story apartment complex was one of several construction projects that had been under the supervision of Nadia's father. Her body had lain at the bottom of the building.

The mother explained to Lexy what had happened. Nadia told her Saturday morning that she would be walking over to a friend's house. By late afternoon, her mother phoned to find out when she would be returning for dinner. She spoke with the girl's mother, who said that her daughter was spending the weekend with relatives, and that she had related this to Nadia when she had stopped by late that morning.

She added that she seemed glum, so she invited her to come inside for a while, but her phone had rung, and Nadia was gone by the time she got back to the front door. By 8:00 that night, her frantic parents phoned the police. The police called them at 3:30 Sunday morning to say that they had found her. Nadia had apparently walked to the building project, about eight miles from her home, climbed the steps to the top level, and jumped.

As the six of us gathered in Lexy's living room that Monday evening before leaving for the parlor, we recalled how depressed Nadia had seemed when we had had dinner with her.

Following high school graduation, several of us had been getting together once or twice a year over a nice dinner. Our latest foray had been a month earlier, at one of the city's finest restaurants. We had often asked Lexy to invite Nadia, but Lexy said she could never get her to come.

Our last dinner marked the first time the rest of us had seen Nadia since high school. It was then that Lexy's words finally sank in. Trying to figure out what went wrong, we remembered that Lexy had occasionally mentioned her hearing problem. Now we began to understand why she was so out of sorts when we were last together. In many restaurants, such as the one we had gone to, the din of plates, clinking glasses, loud voices, and laughter can make hearing difficult, even hearing the person sitting next to you.

We were genuinely interested in what Nadia had been doing all these years, knowing only that she had been living at home and had not been employed. We tried to open up a conversation with her, but she would just shake her head at us in bewilderment.

By the time dinner neared its end, Nadia had assumed an almost belligerent attitude, her arms crossed, finally pushing herself away from the table, walling herself off from us, and everyone around her.

Lexy added, as we left, that Nadia's hearing had gotten so bad that her parents had taken her to a specialist, who said she should be wearing hearing aids. The parents got them for her, but Nadia wouldn't wear them.

We reminisced, too, about our first meeting with Nadia. Her parents had immigrated to the United States from Beirut, Lebanon in the early 1960s.

As a foreigner, she was naturally the center of attention. She was a dark girl, and homely, with a thick Lebanese accent that sometimes made her unintelligible.

Her voice was grating. Even her laughter was raspy, but it was also infectious.

We found it impossible to keep a straight face when she laughed. In the beginning, she laughed often. In time, however, the novelty of Nadia wore off.

She had begun junior high school in the better classes but leveled off to the average ones by graduation

No one seemed to notice her any more. None of us could have fully appreciated then that just as it was difficult for us to understand Nadia, so it was difficult for Nadia to understand us.

I can still see the light outside the funeral home. It was a simple fixture, its light strong but of limited scope, reminding me of a lantern from the days of Dickens, sharpening the contrast between light and darkness.

Uncertain, we quietly opened the parlor's front door and made our way to the room ahead. Perhaps ten people were assembled there, all of them older than us, most of whom appeared to be Mid-Eastern.

A couple standing near the doorway looked at us in surprise as we entered the room. As they approached us, I announced to them that we were Nadia's friends. With that, the man lowered his head, too choked up to speak. The beautiful, tall woman shook my hand and told us that they were Nadia's parents. Holding onto my hand and fighting back tears, she said they were so glad we had come: "It's nice to know that our Nadia had friends after all."

I asked Lexy some years later how Nadia's parents were doing. She said quietly, "Oh, they're gone now. He died a few years later, and she died not long after that." Neither of us could escape the feeling that their daughter's death had hastened their own.

Two months after her death, another Nadia made headlines the world over during the Winter Olympics for her record-breaking 10.0 gymnastics performance. In recognition of her superb accomplishment, a song was released nationwide entitled "Nadia's Theme." It was a lovely and delicate piece with an orchestral background, but it was also a melancholy piece featuring solitary piano notes and an unresolved ending, a song so perfectly suited for a Nadia that no one ever knew.

DOESN'T EVERY SON GET ONE OF THESE LETTERS?
By: Susan Brittain

November 29, 2009

Daniel

I don't think (what with modern communication) that I've ever sat down and written a letter to you, but I don't know how else to explain what is going on in my life. Before I get started I just want to let you know that you and your mother are the most important people in my life and right now I'm thrilled with the path you are taking.

However it's my life that I'm writing about and a journey that I believe I need to take if I am ever to find any inner peace and acceptance for myself and my inner spirit.

Are you sitting down! You are, good then I shall begin.

Since I was first conscious of who I was (probably around 2 or 3 years of age) I have identified as female, which is sometimes described as Gender Identity Disorder or Gender Dysphoria, which according to the medical profession lists the conditions as:

A strong and persistent cross gender identification manifested by a desire to be, to live and to be treated as the other sex.

A persistent discomfort with their bodies.

As a result this causes a significant distress in social, occupational and other areas of life.

It is estimated that about 1 in 30,000 males have this condition (Oh aren't I the lucky one).

So I know the question you are asking is: "What are you going to do about it?"

Have a sex change at 52 years of age? Well not right now but it is the journey that I want to take and explaining to you what is going on is a giant step in that direction.

Daniel I'm exhausted with this fight. I've identified as female since age 3, and my sense of being a women's spirit has never left me. The only time that it vanished was when I fell in love with your mother and when that happened I felt I had been cured by love. I hoped it would be forever but it was not. When you were born I remember holding you and thinking you were the most beautiful thing I had ever held and now I was going to be a man and a father but it didn't last. I grew up in a household of men and went to an all-boys school. I've tried to drink it away and work it away but its there and it will not go away.

So the questions that I wrestle with daily are: am I willing to abandon all the love that has made me whole so that I can enter into a life that I know nothing about? What kind of woman do you think you would be not having grown up as a woman or having a girlhood? What kind of person do you think you would be, leaving Daniel without a father and your mother without a husband? But still?

I know that no amount of wishing this was the case can make it not the case. No amount of praying that I'm not transgendered will make me something other than what I am, and no amount of love from anyone will make me fit inside a body that doesn't match my spirit.

So at 52 I've decided that a lifetime goal has always been to be able to look in the mirror and love the person I'm looking at, to make my outer being fit the inner one.

Just to let you know I haven't lost my marbles. I am working with a wonderful therapist up in Newark, who is helping avoid the pitfalls of walking on an un-trodden path. I'm also married to a wonderful woman who also happens to be a wonderful mother and has had to deal with some aspects of this for a very long time and right now needs all the love and support you can give her.

So where do we stand? I'm no different but I am. This whole process is going to take a while. Right now I've started electrolysis to remove facial hair that might take up to 2 years to finish. I've joined a Transgender Group up in Wilmington (I attended a meeting there 15 years ago) and I've enclosed their newsletter as well as a book if you want to find out more about what is going on. I've a female name "Susan" that I gave myself when I was very young and I still go by. But most of all I just want to be able to talk to you about this.

Daniel right now all I need from you (and that is a gigantic "all") is your unconditional love and understanding even when you feel you can't. I wanted to let you know about this before we came to see you and not drop a bombshell. Also I would ask that for now this stays with you and not get thrown randomly around.

I'm looking forward to seeing you and catching up with what is going on in your life and to spend time

with you and am really looking forward to traveling up to Vancouver with you.

.   I love you

By the time this letter was written in the fall of 2009 I had just turned 52 and Daniel was 23 and my life was about to start unraveling at breakneck speed. Who could believe a letter spanning a few hundred words with few question marks, no exclamation points, and no puddles of blood, sweat and tears could explain my life so simply, but I believe it had.

The story of the person I was had already spanned many continents, many towns, many careers and many unrealized dreams. Even Winston Churchill whose eloquent works on the history of England would not have been able to adequately cover it, let alone make any sense of it.

I placed it in an envelope and put on the required postage (of course it was one of those "Love" stamps that would make the letter so much more compassionate, and easier to understand) and drove it to the post office and dropped it through the slot. The question I now asked myself was: "Is the cement that bonds a family through Joy, Sorrow, Death, Birth, Marriage, and having a Dad who is Transgendered going to shatter and break or just grow more solid?"

I believe more lives are transformed for better or worse by this simple act on a daily basis than all the reported events on NBC, CBS, E-News, etc. I can see the evening news reporting on this; "Transgendered father comes out to son and as a result the Dow drops 200 points and riots have broken out in Baltimore." The newscaster announces. Alas, we who live lives of quiet desperation, just get our report back from the one who receives it a few days later. Some times for the better, some times for the worse but no matter what, the course of our life is changed forever.

I'm in downtown Chestertown a few days later and my phone vibrates and gives a small beep. An incoming text from Daniel. Like a kid opening his report card, or a high school senior looking at his SAT results I click "Open."

"Got your letter. Fantastic. Can't talk now will call."

I break down and cry.

THE GROVE OF PATRIOTS

By: Susan Brittain

The day had started slowly. No parent should have to wake up in the organized chaos of a son's room, but here we were staying with Daniel in Olympia, WA. His room was pleasant enough, but no child's room, even when they are 25 years old, will pass muster for a visiting parent. "Do you need to do laundry Do you need light bulbs? What about clothes?" had been our frequent questions up to now

He was sharing the fourth floor of an old Victorian house in downtown Olympia with two other college grads who all seemed very accepting of two women, Daniel's father and Daniel's mother who had shown up to stay after blazing a trail across Texas, Arizona, California and Oregon in their Subaru Outback.

The day for us to turn back East, and continue our drive across America was drawing near, but breakfast and then a hike was the plan for the day. I slipped quietly out to the bathroom passing Daniel asleep on the floor of the living room. He was, as always showing incredible patience with us and as always I had to also show patience with this wonderful human being who had just two years ago been told that his Dad was going to be his Mum, or something like that.

I had shown up on the doorstep six days ago to greet my son as someone whose inner soul he had known all his life but whose outer appearance he was seeing for the first time. This boy we had raised had somehow been given the gift of unconditional love and that day when I had stepped out of the car he had wrapped his arms around me and let me cry tears of joy. I wanted to sit down next to him and watch him sleep. Somehow in his teenage years this simple privilege had been taken away from us.

He stirred as I walked by and said "Good Morning."

"Hey Dan it's six. You want to get an early start on this hike today? I'll get your mother moving and maybe we can be on the road by seven."

We pulled out of Olympia by seven-thirty and planned to drive around to the southern part of Mt. Rainier and hike up to the "Grove of Patriots." The guidebook had explained it so simply: "A grove of red cedar and Douglas fir trees, some over 1,000 years old." The drive that morning was not quite a scene from a Norman Rockwell painting but close enough. I'm wearing jeans, a fleece and sneakers, not that radical for how society thinks Transgendered women should dress but the small things: a pocketbook, nail polish and jewelry tell the rest of the story. Daniel sits up front with me and Cindy sits in the back. This has been the way we have travelled since Daniel was twelve.

Before I left on this drive across America I had talked to Cindy and Daniel about a small ceremony to welcome Susan to the family and kind of make it official, so that the three of us could move forward as a cohesive unit. The night before we had briefly discussed this and had decided that this might be a good day for this.

We found the base of the hike that we wanted to take and set out on a small steady uphill path. Of course we could have parked at the Grove of Patriots and taken the short hike but our family had already trodden a path rarely taken by many, so heck what difference would an extra couple of hours make. Daniel is the giant of our family and being taller than both of us he led the way. We followed a well-trodden path, with the small signs to tell us we were on track. I wish life did that. Soon we were hiking up through the streams rushing down from Mt. Rainier and the day became beautiful and bright. We made idle talk but mostly we waited for Cindy, the photographer and recorder of our family's history.

We saw no one that early part of the day and fell into a blissful state, with idle chatter and small talk on the back burner. By noon we came to the road that we had to cross and we rejoined a legion of families all hiking the next part of the trail. As we climb up hill, we are passed by families resembling sledding teams. The kids are like huskies baying and howling as they run unchecked ahead up the trail followed by the parents, laden with packs and food and cameras and phones being dragged along by invisible reins bouncing over roots and tree trunks and instead of crying "mush, mush, mush" like an Inuit native they scream "wait, wait, wait," as the teams race to their destination. Ever onward on their own personal "Iditarod Race."

The down-bound traffic is even more entertaining. Hikers with butt cheeks squeezed tight praying for a toilet and please God one that is porcelain and flushes. Little kids who have got halfway up the trail have proven more stubborn than a pack mule and have refused to go further unless returned to the last bathroom stop. And of course the sullen teenager, earplugs in, I Tunes on, and screaming out to the Universe, "Who needs nature?"

The Grove of Patriots is not a circular path but meanders and breaks off and returns and allows us to break away from the traffic and find a place of peace and solace. The trees are magnificent and I am left in total confusion amongst these giants as to our altitude and bearings. I'm doing blond real well today. I'm also realizing that this is going to be a great place to have our ceremony.

Nature knows how to do this so much better than we do. The tree has already been selected and the three of us are drawn to it. Its spirit is ancient and I know it has witnessed or been part of many rituals. This one is going to be a simple release of a spirit.

I start by befriending the tree. I introduce myself and explain my reason for being here today. Transfer of ownership, male to female. The tree sways and rustles in total agreement. "You see Great Spirit that resides here in this sacred place," I say, "Bob needs a place to dwell and roam, but he is a long way from home and I know this is a big favor to ask but could you keep a watchful eye on his spirit?" I know the answer right away for I hug the tree and lay my chest up against its outer bark. I feel Cindy lean up against me and place her hands on the tree and then Daniel lies against us both with his outstretched arms also touching the tree. We cry in unison, great gulps and sobs and gasps for air.

Cindy whispers quietly to the tree, "Bob is a wonderful person but he has almost killed us. He needs release from this pain. We're going to miss him but he needs to make room for Susan in our lives."

I know you are all thinking how could you do something like this. Letting go of a husband, father, son all at once but if this body wants to find any peace in this lifetime Bob needs to roam a free spirit, not trapped in a body that he hated and despised.

The view is great, fresh streams run from the mountains to rivers to the Pacific Ocean and the winds are perfect for sailing. He will be happy here.

I think of the words to the "Ballad of Easy Rider."

"The river flows it flows to the sea, Where ever that river flows that's where I want to be, flow river flow, let your waters wash down, take me from this road to some other town. All he wanted was to be free and that's the way it turned out to be, flow river flow...."

Bob is free and Susan is free. Being a Gemini can be very confusing at times.

We back away from the tree and find a spot by a stream to sit and laugh and smile. We are all radiant. I know Cindy and Daniel are wondering what kind of a woman is Susan going to be. Is she going to be a biker babe, a fashion maven, a sweat pants Mom wearing pajama bottoms and slippers to the mall? Or will she carry herself with dignity and do her family proud?

I stand and raise my arms to the heaven and shout "Look out world here I come and not a minute too late." And we start our climb back down to the lower elevations.

If you're ever hiking around the Grove of Patriots and you come across an Englishman shouting "Hello, Hello. I say old chap, could you tell me what's going on?" Please reassure him that all is well and that he could always head downstream and head for the Ocean where I'm sure he will find passage on a boat bound for China.

THE ADOPTION

By: Barbara Harbeson

    I have a friend named Pam that I met many years ago.

    We were thirty something and both found ourselves in a "Women in Transition" group and it did not take long before we knew that we just wanted to have coffee and be friends. That path led us to our friendship and she shared a story of her pregnancy, back when she was 16 years old.

    Her parents were devout in their religion and they sent her away, to an adjoining state, for the delivery, which was a common practice at that time. There was no discussion of a choice in this matter. The father of the child, Frank, a boy from the high school prom, disappeared as well.

    Life resumed for Pam and she became successful in business and led a creative life, but never married or had any long-term relationships.

    With this discovery she'd revealed to me of her past, I felt she needed to be encouraged to pursue this piece of the puzzle missing in her life, no matter the outcome. I felt it was a proactive move on her part and would help her feel in control of a situation that she had never addressed. So, we sat and wrote a letter to the adoption agency involved. They were located in another state just over the line. She was informed that the letter would be placed on file in the event that the child, a girl, would ever inquire.

It was only six months before a letter and then a call, came to her to say that in fact, her daughter *had* come to inquire and would like to communicate with her. Letters came with pictures and an update of the daughter's life as she was now 20 years old, entering college, had a boyfriend and all of the typical information for her age.

She stated that her father was a builder and that she had an adopted brother as well. They lived at the shore and her name was Megan. I was thrilled for Pam that all of this had come about and looked forward to her learning more about her lost daughter.

Then a phone call came in to her from the agency. They said that the adopted mother did not approve her daughter's search and that the communication would stop until Megan was 21 and could decide for herself. It was obvious that the wings of flight had been clipped. Of course sorrow came over Pam, but I persuaded her to remain hopeful.

The days continue and life goes on and there is little to ponder about this kind of dilemma, because the person who has made this affecting decision is not of like mind. So the only recourse is to hold onto the hope, that "Someday" will come, and so this is what Pam did.

It was just about a year later. I had been dating a nice man and we went to the shore to spend the holiday. On our way home the traffic was very thick and slow and so we decided to make a stop for a while to let some of the traffic clear. He had a friend that lived not too far off the beaten path and that's where we went.

When we arrived, his friend was about to go out on his boat and so they went for a ride on the water as I relaxed on his deck with a glass of wine. While reading my book, I looked up to see that his daughter had arrived. Her name was Megan. She was on a dinner break from her job at the local Crab House. Surprisingly, we had met before and so we began to pick up conversation on the generalities of life. At one point, I paused to say that she must look like her Mother, because she did not have her Dad's tall, thin and very Italian features, hers were more rounded. She stated immediately that she had been adopted at five days old and her brother was adopted as well. I smiled and said that I didn't know that. And suddenly there appeared to be a photograph of Pam's face transposed over the daughter's face almost like a double exposure. I had an eerie feeling and excused myself to the restroom.

Uncertain as how to follow up on this when I returned to the conversation I asked if she had ever had contact with her birth Mother and if she knew her name. The answer was yes on both questions. Megan explained how she had received the information about her birth mother from the agency and she said Pam's name. I was in shock for the moment and then I told her I knew her birth Mother.

The strange revelation of this connection took us both by surprise and we began to cry. Then we hugged as a human response to this unexpected link. At that moment, the boat arrived back at the dock. The men's faces were in bewilderment at our hugs and crying and so Megan told her Father the news of my friendship with her biological Mother. He was not pleased and went pale and stated that it should not come up again.

We left and on the drive home I tried to lay out how I could tell my dear friend that I had met her daughter and how she had chosen to respect her adoptive parent's wishes. Of course, the disappointment was greater than before. Now there wasn't any hope that this dilemma would ever correct itself.

By the fall of the following year, I was getting married and I knew that both Pam, along with her Mother, and also the father of Megan. would be attending. There was stress in my soul over this.

At the wedding, I went to the Father and, taking him by the hand, brought him to the table where his daughter's Mother and Grandmother, were sitting. The resemblance was astounding and as we near the table, I tell him that I want to introduce him to someone, and he looked ahead and remarked, as he saw the two familiar faces, "You won't have to."

The friend of my new husband is respectful of the facts at hand and we were invited to his daughter's wedding, where I took pictures to show Pam. She is pleased to see her daughter's wedding and to know of her happiness through me. Then Megan is pregnant and I take a present to her from her Great Grandmother who made her a blanket for the child to come. No thank you is returned.

You see, the adoptive Mother made the rule for Megan never to see her birth Mother and all had to adhere to her wishes. I bring pictures of the baby and stories too. Some stories I keep to myself as not to hurt Pam. Like the one where, when they were teens, the daughter and her adopted brother worked for the man that I married and that workplace was only five miles from Pam's home where she gave up her baby. Megan was adopted from the adjoining state and then brought back to the neighborhood of her birth Mother.

Pam still has not met her Daughter, and I wonder why?

It is so sad that the need for control on one side truly denies the other.

UNDERTAKING MARGARET

By: Alice Lindsay

I pick up the phone. "Hello?"

Silence.

"Hello? ...Hello? ..."

"Margaret died this morning!"

"What? Oh! It's you, Dad," I say.

"Margaret died? Oh! I'm . . . I'm sorry."

"Yeah," Dad says, his voice cracking.

Margaret was Dad's second companion to die in his five years as a widower. Dad had no trouble finding lady friends. Keeping them alive was another matter. The trouble was Dad, even at age seventy, still preferred girlfriends his senior—a good bit senior. Margaret had been seventy-six, well, not counting the years she didn't count.

Her predecessor, Mary, actually admitted to eighty, before she keeled over with a heart attack.

"I didn't know Margaret had been ill," I say.

"She wasn't. Had a stroke just yesterday. Died this morning. Conscious up to the end but couldn't talk."

"Oh, how sad," I say, trying to sound sympathetic but at the same time wondering what Margaret, not talking, must have been like even for a day. All that weekend she and Dad had spent with us in our little two- bedroom, one bath ranch, Margaret never shut up about that house in Washington.

"Oh, many times the size of this one! A mansion! Five bedrooms, six baths."

On and on she went. A master of the invidious comparison was Dad's Margaret. I learned later she had been the housekeeper and not one of the beautiful people owning that sumptuous abode out of House Beautiful. That weekend was the last time I saw Margaret... alive.

"Do you think you can help me out?" Dad asks in that all-too-familiar "I'm helpless" voice.

"Dad, really!" I protest. "Don't you think you can handle things yourself this time? I know it's hard for you, but Bill and I are just so busy right now." I don't let on how we weren't all that fond of Margaret. But the man is hurting.

"I haven't anyone else I can depend on," he whines. "And Margaret had no family left. It'd only take a couple of days, and, well, I'm just wiped out."

"Oh, all right," I say reluctantly. "I'll call Bill. We can maybe drive up this afternoon. You call Herson. Tell him we'll be in this evening to make the funeral arrangements. You hang in there." I hang up.

"Herson could retire on just your business, Daddy, dear," I mutter and dial Bill.

"Dad's Margaret died this morning," I announce. "A stroke."

"Not again," Bill says with resignation. I ignore the non sequitur.

"I'm afraid I let us in for doing the necessary, again." I say sheepishly. "Don't be mad."

Bill grunts. "Okay! But I wish just once your father could find one of those women who outlive their men. Give me an hour to finish up what I'm doing."

We pick up some Chinese carryout for dinner and arrive at Dad's apartment to find him slumped in his easy chair. He barely whispers, "Hello." I can see he's into one of his "I'm too distraught-you'll-have-to-do-everything-for-me," routines although he's not too upset to polish off most of the rice and General Tso.

"You'll be coming with us to Herson's?" I say, knowing he won't.

"Dear, I really don't feel up to it," he answers. "Don't you think you...?"

"OK, OK," I say, "but you know I don't find conventional funerals exactly death with dignity. Will a closed casket be alright with you?"

"Yeah, sure. Just get the affair arranged," he says absently, as he flips on the TV.

Bill and I head for Herson's Funeral Home, a white pillared mansion on a weeping willow wooded lot, no longer the cramped two room parlor smelling of embalming fluid just across from the railroad tracks where we had had Mary laid out. Mr. Herson is waiting for us. I inform him that we plan on a closed casket.

"Most of our clients prefer to see their loved one," Mr. Herson announces.

"We prefer not to," I say. "May we see the caskets?"

Mr. Herson shows Bill and me into the casket display room. We choose the least expensive number short of an unpainted pine box and make all the other arrangements in the office. The price of the whole deal magically matches the figure of Margaret's insurance. But I wasn't about to haggle. We go back to the apartment. Dad's watching the Pirates defeat the Mets.

"OK, it's all arranged," I tell him over the din of a Pirate's home run. "We'll receive visitors tomorrow afternoon and evening. The service is Tuesday morning. The closed casket made arrangements simple."

"Closed casket!" Dad cries. "Awww! I want to see Margaret."

I should have known. He hadn't been paying attention. I'm in no mood to argue. I get Herson on the phone and change the order to a full layout for Margaret.

"Of course, Mrs. Landry. I understand, Mrs. Landry. No trouble at all, Mrs. Landry," he gloats. "And will you want your . . .your friend in one of our lovely satin slumber gowns?" he oozes.

"Whatever," I answer, rolling my eyes at Bill.

"Of course," he says. "And her feet? Do you want her feet showing? We have lovely slippers to match the raspberry blush of the slumber gown; or do you want her wearing her own footwear—Shoes? Slippers?"

"No shoes, no slippers, just cover the feet." I snap.

"All right, fine," he purrs. "We'll have your . . . your friend ready by noon tomorrow. Your family will of course want an initial viewing before the . . . a . . . the others come in…We'll send the limousine for you and your family at twelve-thirty. Good-night, Mrs. Landry, and be assured, you and yours have our deepest sympathy."

The next morning the traditional casseroles, pastas, pies and cakes start arriving from the neighbors, Dad's "more friends than you can shake a stick at." I recognize the condolatory fare—the same as after Mary's demise. Apple pie from Mrs. Cromby's kitchen—crust made with lard and, tasting, I suspect, not too unlike Mr. Cromby's homemade lard-based soap. And there's my mother-in-law's 'funeral dish,' a watery macaroni and cheese concoction mixed with her not-so-secret ingredient, olives. Mrs. Foster's chocolate layer cake tastes pretty good. No one, except Dad, is all that hungry. The limo arrives.

Mr. Herson is aflutter. He ushers us into Slumber Room #1 where Margaret lies in full cosmetic makeover and mortuary regalia. He gestures toward the corpse with a grand sweep of an arm. Only a fanfare of trumpets is missing. But then Margaret's insurance probably wasn't enough to cover music.

At first Bill and I avoid taking in Mr. Herson's latest masterpiece. Then Dad walks over to look at Margaret. He pulls out his handkerchief and wipes away a tear. I go and put my arm around his shoulder. Bill comes over and stands with us. After awhile Dad puts away the handkerchief and turns to Mr. Herson, who has come up behind us.

"She looks good," he says, "but maybe she oughta have these in? They found them at the hospital," he says, as he pulls Margaret's false teeth out of his coat pocket and tries to hand them to Mr. Herson.

Mr. Herson recoils. He splutters, "Now ... a...that could be a bit of a problem. Actually, don't you think she looks natural just the way she is ... that is . . .?"

Familiar with Jessica Mitford's The American Way of Death I know Margaret's mouth is wired shut, and it would probably be a big logistic undertaking to get it open and re-shut. Without commenting on how natural or unnatural Margaret looks with her mouth just as it is, I get Mr. Herson off the hook.

"It's not important, Dad. She looks fine," I say.

Dad grunts and slips Margaret's teeth back in his pocket. Mr. Herson busies himself with placing a basket of gladiolas just arrived from Teamsters' Local #10, Dad's union buddies. Dad had scotched "The family requests, in place of flowers..." idea too. Friends drop by throughout the afternoon and evening with their commonplace but well-meaning condolences:

"My, doesn't she look nice?"

"So natural. You'd think she's just asleep."

"She'll be missed."

I can deal with these, but I'm not sure what to say to the elderly gentleman who stands looking at Margaret while nodding and repeating at intervals, "Yes . . . Yes . . . Yes . . ." He fails to elaborate on these affirmatives. Finally I say as philosophically as I can, "Yes." And, not surprisingly, he agrees.

I'm struggling to think of something more to say to the Assenting Stranger when a commotion in the foyer draws my attention. Then all of a sudden Dad's next-door neighbor, Joe, on a run, bursts into Slumber Room #1. Dropping to his knees, like a figure skater, Joe slides about two feet across the polished hard wood floor and comes to rest in front of the casket. Clutching a rosary to his chest, he shouts, "Hail Mary! Hail Mary! Hail Mary!" He then stands up as abruptly as he had knelt and goes over to Dad to offer, I assume, a more conventional expression of sympathy.

I look around for Yes Man, but he's gone. I realize visiting hours are coming to a close when I see a circle of mourners gathered around my mother-in-law getting up and saying their good-byes. I suspect she has been telling them how it had been one of the great disappointments in her life not to have worked in a funeral home as a greeter steering visitors to coat racks, rest rooms, or where ever. Visiting hours are over... mercifully.

When we arrive at Hersons the next morning, my mother-in-law, several handkerchiefs at the ready, is already ensconced in the front row of folding chairs facing the casket. A few visitors go up to say a last good-bye to Margaret and, God forbid, kiss the corpse. Mr. Herson ushers Dad, Bill and me into Grief Room #1, a side chamber to Slumber Room #1 intended to provide special privacy for relatives of the deceased.

The service begins. Margaret's minister, it turns out, is on vacation, so his friend, Dr. Grove, a clergyman of advanced years and unfamiliar with Margaret and the rest of us, gives the eulogy. He's not good with names. But we assume the "Dear Friend" he mentions a couple of times refers to Dad, and he does manage to resurrect Margaret's name just prior to giving the benediction.

Four of Dad's Teamster buddies and a couple of Herson's hired pallbearers close the casket and carry the encased Margaret to the waiting hearse. Mr. Herson ushers us to the waiting limousine, and we're off to the cemetery.

101

The burial is routine. No one breaks down. Reverend Grove remembers all of his lines and even gives a nice reading to the first few verses of "Abide with Me." The funeral is over.

Bill and I thank the dozen or so people for coming and saunter over toward the limousine.

Dad stops to chat then catches up. He's found a friend.

"I'd like you to meet Irene Williams," Dad says, presenting a plump elderly lady in a blue rinse under a wide brimmed black hat swathed in black veiling. "We met at the Senior Center last month. Her husband passed away about a year ago. She saw Margaret's death notice in the paper."

"Hello, Irene, nice to meet you," I say.

"Likewise, I'm sure," she replies.

"Irene invited me to ride back in her car. We thought we might stop for a drink."

"Oh, OK," I say. "We'll just go back in the limo by ourselves."

We watch the two friends walk away. Dad slips his arm around Irene's shoulder.

Bill chuckles. "How long do you figure that's going to last?"

I smile. "Let's hope for a really long time...for their sake."

Bill smiles and nods. We head for the limo.

POEMS

By: Virginia Coleman

Drought

Stalks of corn in orderly rows
Roots planted in hard-parched ground
Broad leaves piped in protection from
Glare of hot piercing sun
Mute supplication for life sustaining rain
Flashes of light on the horizon
Deep mutters of thunder growl in the distance
The dark sky lowers
A breeze races across the forming tassels
And rustles the waiting leaves
The flashes and muttering ceases
As the wind flees to tease another field
No rain answers the silent prayer

Landscape

In springtime appears a delicate shimmer
Tender green or rosy pink
Leaves of trees start to form
Fragrant blossoms beckon *Look at me*
Even during the dark of night

Summer brings soothing green foliage
Cool luxurious relief from hot sun
Space to pause and consider the gift

A jubilation of color showering down
On cool, crisp days of fall
The world afire in red and gold
Sated with abundance

Winter reveals the majestic framework
Now stripped bare to gray and brown
The landscape larger, more lonely
Without the tree's decorative garb

Flirt

Spring is the sexy starlet of seasons
Golden glow and flirtatious smile
Suggestive promise of good times to come
Lushly abundant possibility
How enticing to bask in
her voluptuous warmth.

Shades of Night

Pale gray darkens the blue sky
Mothers call children from play
A bird sends up the last joyful song of the day
As darkness creeps over the yard
And envelops the house

Weary workers turn into the drive
A rustle of feathers and soft twitters from the
pine tree, as porch lights say welcome home
A telephone ring promises plans for the evening
Children damp and sweet from the bath beg for
one more story
Street lamps cast islands of light and safety

The night grows dark and still
Deep sleep of an exhausted laborer
A solitary sleeper where two had cuddled the
month before
Whispered promises betrayed in light of day

Tossing and turning among rumpled sheets and
hot pillows
Nighttime terrors of unclaimed fears and guilt

The silent passage of the moon overhead
Quiet prayers drifting upward
Sweet relief of sleep

PUNXSY PHIL RULES IN NORTHWEST PENNSYLVANIA

By: Linda Garman-Weimer

Yes, Virginia, there is a Punxsutawney before and after Groundhog Day, February 2. But the creature, also called a woodchuck, seems to run things in this Pennsylvania town of 6,000 year round.

During my recent visit I asked a librarian in the downtown library, "What goes on in Punxsutawney when it's NOT groundhog season?"

"It's always groundhog season in Punxsy." she said, using the town's common nickname. And my subsequent visit proved her right as this small town, 84 miles northeast of Pittsburgh, about 7 hours from Chestertown, is so based on the furry rodent that there are five-foot statues of him almost everywhere you look –

*In front of the public library.
*Outside the modern, attractive high school
*In front of the downtown weather museum -
The Weather Center -that's designed for kids but fun for adults too.
*In an empty space along the main drag.
*In a welded, modernistic version on Gobbler's Knob, the nearby mountain top where the official ceremony and weather verdict take place

attended by scores of media and weather buffs seated in an outdoor amphitheater.

The traditional event includes a late-night bonfire to help stay warm in climate about 20 degrees colder than the Eastern Shore. Some fans stay all night, waiting for Punxsutawney Phil's emergence.

Of course, the reason for all this hubbub is the old folk superstition that on this day, Candlemass on the Christian calendar, the stocky brown animal predicts either an incipient spring or six more weeks of winter. Cloudy weather is a good omen in this case; if Phil sees no shadow, spring is around the corner.

The official sponsor, the Groundhog Club, has an attractive website, groundhog.org, with a frequently asked question page that suggests you won't get any straight answers. I was curious whether the club sponsors a groundhog farm somewhere to make sure that some Phil or other emerges from his burrowed stump. Although zoology experts say the creature, the most widespread marmot in North America (Louisiana to southern Alaska) lives only to a maximum of 10 years in captivity (4-6 years in the wild), the club claims that there has been one and only one Phil since 1887 – and that he gets his longevity from a potion administered every fall that guarantees another seven years of health.

At the Weather Center, there's an interesting scrapbook on how the observation has grown over the years since 1887, when the whole thing started as a groundhog hunt for the purpose of a groundhog feast. The seer seems to make decent eating too. This shouldn't surprise an Eastern Shoreman who has chowed down on a traditional local dish about the same time of year – the muskrat.

However, don't look for locations from the classic 1993 movie "Groundhog Day," starring Bill Murray and Andie MacDowell. That was filmed in Woodstock, Ill. Still, the scrapbook at the Weather Center contains some shots of the production. The changed location may be due to the fact the town is an old industrial center, once heavily dependent on coal, and not the most attractive of places.

The main drag, Mahoning Street, has a few stylish places, in particular a stained glass shop and an assortment of older-type businesses like hardware. And there are several reasonable, homey places to have a meal.

But the problem for visitors traveling from Chestertown is the lack of attractive lodging in the heart of things. I stayed just outside downtown in a dated motel called the Country Villa; clean enough but barely tourist class even at the great rate of $45 per night. The downtown hotel, the Pantel, has "poor to fair" ratings on two of three online reviews.

There is also a B&B five easy miles from town, the Jackson Run Bed and Breakfast, which looks appealing on its website but offers only three rooms and a separate cottage.

For more amenities and more rooms, it appears you'd need to stay in the town of Indiana, about 30 miles to the south on Route 119, which has a Comfort Inn, or north in DuBois.

I didn't use the directions given on the Chamber of Commerce's website, punxsutawney.com, but took a road trip the old-fashioned way, with a road map. This circuit took me off the PA Turnpike at Rte. 220 North, and then on Interstate 99, West on Rte. 422, which gave me dramatic views of wind farms along the ridges.

Finally, I met the main road into town from the south, Rte. 119. It was well worth the extra miles.

MOVING ON
By: Ronny Aseltine

So, there she stood, in this tiny space within a large room, smushed in by six-foot-high metal shelves filled with boxes. Well, some plastic containers, some boxes, and lots of random items that had been unceremoniously dumped when she, or Rich, had wanted to get something out of the way.

All of this, she thought, *represents my life. My past sits in here along with that of my husband and my son and some of my mother's things, plus belongings from my in-laws, my sister and my brother. What a lousy mess.* She recalls hearing of a book titled "Does This House Make Me Look Fat?" *I could write one titled "Does This House Make Me Look Insane?"* she thought. She was not certain that insane covered the subject, but she certainly felt overwhelmed and sad as she looked around.

What is this, she asks herself? She turns and, as she does, her arm grazes an ill-placed box and its contents spill out. Ineffectually she tries to grab the falling papers. Now, looking down at the fallen pages, she sees her mother's slightly torn and yellowing sketches lying on the floor. Her heart hurts. She picks them up and replaces them in the box. *"Oh way to go, that's really taking care of it,"* she tells herself as she closes the box and puts it on the floor.

As she heads for the door she stops and touches some of the books that had belonged to her son. She gazes up at the many toys stacked, still in the original boxes he had insisted on keeping as each gift was received. Her mind wanders back to images of long ago Christmases. She sees herself anxiously watching him open a gift, hoping that getting this right would balance against all the times she got things wrong. *Oh well that was then and this is now, so Miss Thing, what are you going to do about this room and how are you going to do it?*

She slouches out of "the room" in search of a cup of coffee. When in doubt, have a cup of coffee, she tells herself bitterly. She decides to reassure herself by looking at the rest of the house. This house had been built in 1896 by a banker for his growing family and by the time she and Richard got it in 1995, it was in need of restoration and un-muddling. Some houses have been remodeled, some have been restored and others re-muddled. This one had suffered some re-muddling but not to the degree that many other homes in the village had endured.

She and Rich had purchased the house with the intention of restoring it and over the years they had become addicted to watching "This Old House" and reading the same named magazine. Over a long period, while spending too much money and too much time, they had been able to lovingly restore the house with period appropriate finishes, with one exception. She did not recover the walls with the beautiful but dark and busy wallpapers that had originally been applied. Instead they had the plaster refinished and most of the interior rooms in the house had been painted butter yellow in a fairly successful attempt to offset the long dark Vermont winter days.

But enough with the Martha Stewart angle; her problem is this room, at the back of the house. It was filling her head like a nightmare from which she could not wake. Just thinking about this room made her anxiety level rise and gave her that hot poker feeling in her gut.

What in the hell is wrong with you, she asks herself. *Just go in there and deal with it. Just do it.* Fortunately she hears the doorbell and runs downstairs to open the door. Her friend Julie is there.

"Julie!" she cries, "Can you stay for tea, or coffee, and a psychotic episode? "

"Sure," she answers, "I'm just on my way home from the chiropractor and I thought I d stop by. What's wrong with you, Nicky, have you been crying?"

Had I been crying she thought? *I guess I have been* she acknowledged but she had not realized it. How ridiculous.

Over coffee Nicky describes her dilemma to Julie, who listens skeptically as she tells her about what she has come to think of as "the room." They go upstairs to view the subject of her distress. When she opens the door, Nicky feels like she is ripping a Band-Aid off a wound.

"Oh," Julie says, "It's not that bad" and they both burst out laughing.

Nicky thinks: *you have to love your friends, don't you?*

"What does Rich say?"

"Oh he thinks we should just let the movers pack it up and deal with it later"

"I hate to tell you," Julie admits, "But that is just what I would do."

Julie is an amazing artist and friend for all reasons and seasons, but she is a pack rat in her own right and half her Christmas decorations are still up. *Though Julie is a great person to vent with, maybe she is*

113

not the best person to advise me, in ways that I can handle on this situation, Nicky tells herself.

Ok, I need to talk to Carole who is an old friend and also my realtor, Nicky decides. She noticed that Carole, while viewing the house when she was measuring for dimensions, had not said a word when she got to the room. Though Carole had been to her home many times for dinner or parties, Nicky couldn't remember having her upstairs so she had never seen it before.

Nicky calls Carole. Carole asks her when she wants the listing to go up.

"Well," Nicky says, "I need to deal with the storage room first."

"Thank God you said that," Carole sighs, "I was afraid to bring it up. What is going on in there?" Nicky tries to explain. Finally Carole makes her suggestion.

"Honey, almost all houses have some version of that room. Usually it's in the attic or the basement. Just order a dumpster and hire someone to haul all that stuff out of there, it will be over before you know it."

"That's an idea." Nicky responds

Hearing that most people have some out of control space in their home makes her feel better but the hire-someone-and-a-dumpster idea makes her feel even worse.

"Watch that show about house cleaning," her neighbor, Penny, suggests.

"They have a show about house cleaning?" Nicky asks.

"Oh yeah, a whole bunch of them, I'll e-mail you the names and channels."

Why am I surprised to hear about a show that focuses on house cleaning? Nicky asks herself. *They have shows about people with dozens of children, people who hunt crocodiles, pregnant teenagers, people getting divorces, people working on cars, people getting tattoos, beauty pageant children, people trying to design clothes, so I guess the American public will watch a show about cleaning houses.*

The next day she is glued to the television, watching people who cannot walk through their homes because of clutter, being lectured by a man with an Australian accent. He is telling them that they deserve better. They cry and explain and resist. There are actually two or three different productions.

Nicky watches these shows with the horror and fascination of someone watching a car crash. *Well I'm not like that,* she tells herself. *Except for "the room," my house is photographable.*

She continues to watch these shows. Her husband watches a few of them with her. He thinks the people on the shows are crazy people and he thinks she is demented for watching them. He leaves the room shaking his head.

This goes on for a few weeks. Finally, she hears something that sort of pings with her. A woman is standing there crying over a ceramic dinksbump that her mother made for her when her child was born. It's chipped and cracked because it has been badly stored. Nicky realizes that the woman on the show is feeling the same sorrow she feels about those badly stored drawings lurking up in "the room."

Now that she has whined and complained to everyone she knows about her room, and watched hundreds of people deal with the clutter bombs in their homes, she feels ready to take action. But she needs a plan of attack.

She consults with her sister. Off they go to purchase lots of clear plastic bins in a size she can manage, also contractor grade trash bags and several boxes of tissue.

On the morning of the day the war is to commence, she has breakfast with her friends and her sister at the local diner. They all hug, before she marches off into the breach. Her resolve is that she will attack one three- foot area today and then she will retreat, evaluate, and plan the next day's effort.

Over the coming days she does battle with herself, her past, her dreams, her hopes and her stuff. At first she does more crying than cleaning.

"My son touched this," she sobs, and *"Richard wore this tie at our wedding."*

More weeping, ensues as she moves the items from one pile of indecision to another. She continues to weep and wail through the entire day, and well into the second and third. *"What is it that I am crying about?"* she asks herself over and over again. She has no specific answer.

Finally her focus begins to change, and she begins to find herself coming to terms with the many thoughts and feelings that she, like Scarlett O'Hara, had put aside to think about tomorrow.

As she makes decisions about what is really important and worthy of space in her life, she begins to make some degree of peace with herself over the disparities between what she thought should happen in her life, and what did happen. And the fact that, though she wished she had been a perfect mother, daughter, wife, sibling and person, keeping all this stuff will not change what she had-or had not-done.

116

I'll just have to attain perfection in another life, she tells herself.

Some things leave in contractor trash bags. Some things are carefully packed away so that when she is a grandmother she will have lots of great books and toys, as well as a complete Brio train set, for the grandchildren.

She whittles down her must-have memorabilia to two containers. Some things go with her sister, who has volunteered to take things to Goodwill. She starts to spend more time reflecting on her better moments and happiest memories and the things she is looking forward to.

She lets the failures, the shouldas, the couldas and the wouldas exit the building right along with contractor trash bags.

She goes back to the box that holds the drawings that her mother made of them when they were very young children.

She remembers thinking that they were beautiful when she first saw them. She had been six years old and she could recall coming home from school one day and seeing these charcoal sketches of her brother and sister and herself. It was the first time that she really saw her mother as someone other than her mom.

In that moment she realized that her mother really was an artist, a term she had heard, but never related to her mommy. Nicky was fascinated by the drawings and she thought they were beautiful. These sketches were preliminary studies for paintings that were never painted. They were never displayed, just shut away in a box that eventually landed in "the room" along with letters and documents her mother had put aside for consideration at some other point in time.

117

She takes these drawings and has three sets matted and framed, one for herself and a set for both of her siblings. The three of them have birthdays within weeks of one another, so usually they have one celebration of their personal new year together. This year they are celebrating their birthdays, for the last time, in this house.

This house is where her son grew to adulthood, where her mother spent her final years, where her sister got married, and where her brother came to recover from both heart attacks.

This is the place where birthdays and Thanksgivings and Christmases were celebrated, where so many community meetings were held, and where friends were entertained.

Nicky presents her sister and brother with a set of these framed pictures as a gift from her and from their recently deceased mother.

These pictures capture something of the best part of their childhoods. They show her mother's eye for the beauty and uniqueness she saw in each of them.

These pictures display her talent and the love that this woman, who would soon succumb to a mental illness that would disrupt their lives completely, had for them.

Dear Sibs, she wrote.

I am getting ready to move hundreds of miles away. Time and space will separate us but these pictures, our shared memories and moments-like this birthday-are our anchors. They are a kind of symbolic place marker to have and remember as we face our successes and our stumbles, our past and our futures, wherever we may be.

Love Always and Always,

Nicky

NIGHT ENTRY

By: Alice C. Cory

Now I lay me down to sleep...

With a sigh I open the nearby medicine cabinet and reach for my toothbrush. Why is this stray line from a long forgotten childhood prayer worming its way through my brain? It must be a by-product from tonight's weariness.

It's been decades since thinking about this youthful plea to higher powers. How did it go? Oh, I remember now:

> *Now I lay me down to sleep*
> *I pray the Lord my soul to keep*
> *If I should die before I wake*
> *I pray the Lord my soul to take*

I wonder if children still recite it as their last act before light's out for the night. With an invisible power of its own, this thought grabs me and we scamper back to distant younger times.

Mine - childhood, that is - was programmed with predictable proprieties and routines by my mother whose days and nights were grounded in rituals, superstitions, and energetic attempts to infuse them into those around her. Some of her more innocent beliefs included the presence throughout our home of small pink ceramic elephants with raised trunks, preferably studded with rhinestones, to ensure prosperity; and eating dried herring on New Year's Eve to guarantee something or other which I've long since forgotten. Nighttime prayers to prevent dream visits from those who had died were a top priority.

At some point growing up, I've convinced myself Mom's practices provided her with a sense of security in a world not necessarily under her control. If nothing more, it's a logical explanation for what seemed illogical. For a while, I hoped she was trying to protect a little-understood daughter. Oh, if I could only believe that, the memory would leave a warmer imprint but I gave up trying to remake history's baggage into silk long ago.

Another sigh escapes along with my overused mental mantra, "*She was doing the best she could but I was too young to understand.*" Crap, here comes the guilt again! The truth is, she and I never connected in the way she craved, but she finally did accept a compromise with evening prayers. I insisted upon and she gave in to just one prayer from her endless menu of choices. One and no more! And now those well-worn words are rattling back from the past.

It's much more fun to recall my practical father's recommendations regarding nightly requests from God, angels, and anything else pertaining to the mysterious higher domains. He preferred focusing on blocking undesirable possibilities rather than appealing for protection from the powerful positives. His consistent advice of: "Alice, whatever you say and do, make sure it goes up and not the other way," resonated within me perhaps due to its own rhyming cadence. Or was it his timely way of looking upward when saying "up" followed by a dramatic flourish of thumbs down when ending with "the other way"?

Regardless of his sound reasoning, my focus in those formative years was more on keeping my mother at bay since the devil and dark forces seemed the lesser challenge. And so, her prayer became my nightly mindless habit.

Thinking back to my deceased parents, a long-married yin-yang couple in whose life I was thrust by some warped sense of cosmic humor, leaves its usual whiff of bafflement. Their only common interests were a love for Skunk Cabbage, apparently for health and longevity, along with their immense fear of owls, which were supposedly messengers of destruction or death. The balance of their leisure time was spent in good-natured bickering about the relevant and the not so.

Even though they lived into their 90's, providing arguable support for their practices, I was and remain a contrarian daughter who neither shares the need for bedtime prayer rituals nor enjoys the taste of cabbage. And then there's my lifelong love for owls, big and small, and their haunting hoots from the nearby woods.

Fortunately, both parents died without ever knowing the depth of my differences from them, particularly one secret that would have bound their fears together much tighter than food or flying creatures. Only my maternal grandmother knew of my frequent seeing and hearing 'people' who, she claimed, others could not detect and would have become frightened if they had.

Early photos of almost five feet tall Gramma Minnie reflect a beautiful, softly smiling, and relaxed woman, but by the time I was growing up, she was sadly withdrawn. Although we lived in the same house with my parents for the first fifteen years of my life, I never really knew her and many times have wished that were different. But we shared one secret and that was about the otherworldly visitors I routinely saw.

When the first visit occurred, I was three years old; Gramma Minnie and I were thankfully alone. As she listened to my excited tale, she gave me my first lesson in life's complicated labyrinths. With her hands on my little shoulders, our noses almost touching, she calmly made me promise never, ever to tell anyone else. "This secret is ours; only for the two of us," she whispered.

As a child, it wasn't hard to honor our mutual oath since my invisible visitors seemed normal within my young world, but a secret with this gently quiet woman made them special and exciting. Looking back, it's oddly understandable that it was our shared promise rather than the mysterious visits, which proved more important to my development.

I was an adult before I fully understood the extent of protection she granted through her wise advice on this topic. As Mom and Dad aged, they talked more and more about their overwhelming terror of death and the possibility that the living could be visited by those who have already passed. Their daughter's confirming the existence of the latter would not have helped!

Gramma has long ago passed but my deep love for her and her three life-long gifts linger. Through her example, she showed me daily how to be a very, very good secret keeper and by keeping her word, she taught me how to trust. She took our secret to her grave. Because of her, I still seek deep-seated integrity within a person rather than care about their facade and life's experiences--glitzy or mundane. Her third lesson of teaching much by saying very little still eludes me.

That child I was is long gone. My youthful abilities to see and hear our many non-form visitors faded as adolescence turned into adulthood, marriage, and all that comes with it. My last remaining souvenir from those earlier times is seeing morning and night energy movements. Every once in a while I look back to the long ago haunting visits with nostalgia, wondering what happened to those who wandered into my physical space and time. Or did I wander into theirs?

Returning to the now with a jolt from this rare detour down memory lane, I find myself squeezing toothpaste into the sink while my toothbrush is quietly resting where I evidently dropped it onto the floor. Pre-bed prep suddenly seems an obstacle to much preferred blanket snuggling. So I'll do just what my childhood prayer suggests--head to pillow without further preamble.

My bedroom is truly a silent and safe sanctuary. With curtains and door closed, it is completely and darkly, well, *dark*. Each night I lie within this comforting cave watching the slow emergence of energies swirl and sway across the ceiling. Accompanied by an owl chorus, bedtime takes on a mystical mantle; my current version of connection with whatever Greater Power may be.

So on this Spring May night I nestle in, pulling the covers up to my chin while noticing the usual nightly hums and hoots are strangely silent. Childhood memories are tucked away while hoping for restful sleep after a draining day.

With no warning, a gentle glow immediately arises kitty-corner from me, upon the long wall running to my right. From the floor it unfolds smoothly and quickly, expanding simultaneously both upward and outward with no explainable source. I raise myself onto my right elbow to get a better look at this puzzling phenomenon and reach with my left hand to pinch my right forearm. Ouch! Yup, I'm awake.

In addition to this even occurring at all, the oddity of it is enhanced by the glow's distinctly defined shape, somewhat like an enormous door. Since the ceiling is raised in this portion of the house, I'm guessing its height is now almost twelve feet with its width retaining appropriate door-like proportions.

I take a deep breath. Did my nostalgic wandering a few minutes ago trigger something in the here and now? What in heck is this and, with no source of light, how can it be happening?

As the oblong shape stops its growth spurt as quickly as it started, a dark form glides through it into my room and stops, silhouetted against the light. This latest addition's huge mass explains the size of the now proven to be passageway. It-he-she-whatever has no recognizable features or appendages such as head, arms, legs, but does stand upright resembling a giant under a black fluid covering. Other than its immense size, it could be a child dressed on Halloween as a black sheet-covered ghost. Much like us, this visitor is slightly smaller at the top with a flare of bulk toward the middle, which carries through to the floor.

Astonished, bewildered, yet extremely curious, I hold my breath for a few seconds and automatically tune into my intuition just as I learned to do long ago. Now what?

Breathe; again, breathe; engage mind; breathe. There's no sense of panic, just the desire to understand and touch into whatever is happening. I scramble through distant memories for any similar youthful meeting but come up blank. It doesn't resemble anyone or anything

126

from those days. I exhale a silent "*Ohhhhhh*" while frozen in fascination.

Sensing neither danger nor negativity, I tentatively send a soft energy toward this visitor. In seeming response, it turns its full form toward me as though attempting a clearer view of me just as I'm doing with it. Slowly gliding in my direction, it stops halfway between its lighted backdrop and me. Movements are smooth as though propelled on silent wheels while its turning lacks the jointed characteristic of our bodies.

We are now two beings doing what? Sizing each other up? Deciding the other is rather odd looking? Making friends?

And then I feel its gentle whisper of warm, soft energy touch upon me, flowing down my body erasing all earlier fatigue, leaving only a sense of peace. It is both restorative and surprisingly familiar. Did we know each other during some other time or is it merely a polite acknowledgement as we literally pass in the night?

The form then turns to my left, glides into the darkness that lies away from its entry portal, and passes from my sight. *"Noooooo, don't go."* I silently call after it. The soft glow upon the wall fades much as it had unfolded.

Feeling both wonder and awe, I lay back staring at the corner where it all started. But what IS it that started? And then the questions start tumbling together.

Who or what just shared a few moments of its existence in, of all places, my bedroom? Where is it traveling from and to and why? Will I see the visitor's return back through the same doorway? Does it even intend to return? Is it a scout of one or one of many?

So many questions, with no answers; none at all. An uneasy sense that a rare opportunity is missed now lies like an overly heavy blanket. Why didn't I try speaking with it? Why! This repeats within me like a frozen recording as I stare upward.

The questions with their mysteries mingle with the energy movements beginning their evening dance on the ceiling and will, like them, remain unknown and unanswerable.

Since the energy received from this being felt lovingly curative, it seems absurd to doubt that the visit has anything other than a positive purpose, but what is it? I concentrate on relaxing and gradually my emotions morph into a deep heartfelt longing to understand more. If thoughts are, as some claim, an energetic force that can lead to concrete results, is it possible that I can touch upon that being again; or will it touch upon all of us once it knows we're ready?

If this stranger has wisdoms or ancient truths to share, please let it linger in our earthly world and may there be many more entering through various locations. Is that so preposterous? Perhaps if they stay long enough we can re-connect with their teachings from which we've undoubtedly strayed and forgotten. So much hope lies within this one thought.

Everything remains silently dark until the first owls hoot sounds somewhere in the quietness of forested time.

I slide into sleep, hearing my childhood prayer whispering anew.

Now I lay me down to sleep
Teachings in my soul to steep
If I should die before I wake
May this memory never forsake.

POEMS

By: Joe Cullis

I'm in the middle of a world
One that does not care
If I am living my heart beating
Or if I'm lying dead somewhere
The wind of change around me blows
It does not care
If I am living my heart beating
Or if I'm lying dead somewhere
My stench away it will carry
You'll see it does not care
If I am living my heart beating
Or if I'm lying dead somewhere
The world around me
like a weed grows
Up and around me
Soon it will cover me
It simply does not care
That I am living my heart beating
Or if I'm lying dead somewhere
Under my feet
Is barren ground
I know it does not care
If I am living my heart beating
Or if I'm lying dead somewhere
When I am gone the weed continues
You see it did not care
That I was living my heart beating
And now I'm lying dead somewhere

Even in this world
I can find a bit of hope
Even in this world I fear
I can find a bit of hope
Even in this place
I have found a friendly face
Even in this world I hate
A corner I have found
And a melancholy friendly smile
Even in this world
I can find a bit of hope
A bittersweet and sad embrace
In my corner
Safe with you
Even in this world I fear
I can find a bit of hope
Because you have made me smile

I scream at you
I shout at you
I hit you
I laugh at you
I lean on you
And cry
And through all this
You do nothing
You are cold
Cold and hard
Giving in to nothing
And no body
You don't react
To anything
You're a damn wall
A brick wall
Is there nothing
That can break you
Nothing that can fell
Just one brick
From your hard face
Will nothing bring you down
Or make you crumble
Will I always lean on you
And cry

Top of stove directions:
Just add water
Stir in contents of package
Instant lemon flavor
Kitchen tested
Whole grain enriched
Naturally sodium free
Naturally refreshing
Contains less than 2 %
Of the U.S. RDA
Of these ingredients
The highest quality available
We value your feedback
Garnish if desired
High altitude directions
No adjustments necessary
Our seal. Your assurance
Of quality and performance
Any questions or comments?
The refrigerator has
No secrets

My heart and soul
Is ripped
Torn
Into tiny pieces
And tossed
From a mountaintop
To scatter
Like confetti
Across prairies
Forests
And to the sea
Come see
The show
Laugh at
The spectacle
Gawk at
My nakedness
As I am exposed
Every vanity
Ripped away
Come watch
Come cry
Come stand
By my side
If you can

**Title Poem from my book. "Drowning
In My Tea Cup"**

The water
Freshly drawn
Saved from the boil
By seconds
And just filling the mug
Is already stained
Delicately browned
By the hydrating leaves
A fine pekoe
To stimulate thoughts
And warm spirits
Of a delicately flavored
Rapport
Loosing time
And finding a friend
Drowning together
In the depths
Of a tea cup

CHILDISH RANT

By: Virginia Coleman

Why are we in today's society so obsessed with hurrying children along their paths in life? It seems we are constantly pushing or encouraging them to act older than their age. We don't allow them time to be children, to explore, to question, and to dream.

Walk into any children's clothing department and it is depressing to see the displays on shelves, hangers, and in shoeboxes. Baby clothes in animal prints and neon colors with logos and questionable phrases printed on many. Training bras and high-heeled shoes for nine-year-olds are abundant. Clothing for little girls lean toward streetwise tart. For boys, the clothing is baggy, oversized, and prolific with pictures and slogans better not seen. Why do we allow or encourage this wise-mouth and suggestive way of dressing for our youngest and most innocent?

By age three, children are in organized playgroups and by five they are in school, learning T-ball, taking dance, swimming, and skating lessons with never a moment to spare and often too little rest. They are up early, off to daycare or school followed by afternoons of lessons and activities for themselves and siblings. Their daily schedules are more packed than those of many corporate executives. The worst thing imaginable is that the child is not constantly directed and entertained. When do they have time to discover what they enjoy doing or to entertain themselves or to discover that solitude is sometimes to be savored. I hear a constant refrain from children in stores, on sidewalks, and at the beach - "BORING." This word obviously strikes fear in the hearts of all parents or children wouldn't use it so frequently.

Today's child experiences graduation so many times the word has no meaning. They are graduated from Pre-K to elementary school, to middle school, and to high school. What feeling of achievement accompanies these regroupings on the way to the final completion of a required course of study? Graduation should mean staying the course, achieving the goal of finishing the upward climb necessary to earn a diploma.

School dances now begin in the third and fourth grades. The middle school prom is on par with the Miss America pageant. Recently it was reported that the average cost of attending a high school prom is seven to eight hundred dollars. This includes attire, limousine, flowers, dinner, and after prom party. It may not include a day at the spa to ready the young lady's hair, nails, and skin for the evening of enchantment. Many older couples could attest that their weddings cost less and the enchantment still lingers, regardless of the modest investment to prepare for the event.

By the time they are sixteen, too many young people are jaded. They need constant entertainment and stimulation. They have been everywhere and done everything and of course, as true since time began, know everything. Unfortunately, many have had little time to get to know themselves, to eat as a family around the dinner table, and to learn to become self-starters and team players.

With our help, they did not have time to learn the lessons of childhood because they were focused on being grown up.

TUMBLEWEEDS

By: Frances Reed

I measure my forward progress in life by the amount of dust and dust bunnies that surround me. The fewer dust bunnies, the greater my progress. Sadly, so far, my progress is painfully slow. Actually, it's close to non-existent. The dust and dust bunnies in my life definitely have the edge. I always mean to do well, to have the house spick and span and dust free so I can sit down and write in perfect harmony with my house, my family and my world.

It isn't going to happen.

That realization came to me, just now, whilst walking through my living room, past the four sleeping dogs and then again when I stopped to look about me.

Lurking under the table are ephemeral tufts of dog hair that run away from my broom and dodge the vacuum cleaner hose, floating away to hide under the couch until I am gone. Everywhere are books, mostly mine, covering all available surfaces.

My tidy husband has the one book he is currently reading, sitting on the table next to his chair. His books, waiting to be read, are stacked neatly on the mantelpiece, next to the books he has already read.

Periodically he clears out the read ones, donating them or putting into my little antique store to sell. He likes blood and guts books and movies. Not mysteries but "Save the World, Save America!" preferably with a bloody trail of bodies. I once skimmed one and counted at least 17 dead people by the end and those all killed by the hero. There were just as many more killed by the villain. Definitely a form of fictional, population control for the author(s) as they go on, in their subsequent books, to do it again, and again.

I marvel anew at the pleasure it gives my husband to read these books and then realize - *his* mess is all *inside* the books he reads, unlike my mess that seems to be growing daily all around me.

I like books with happy endings for my fiction but I don't think there is room in my brain for any more romances and prowling the living room, I realize reading fiction is not part of my life style any more. All I see are books about fabric, sewing, fashion, roses, gardening, painted furniture and books on writing, spilling across tables, stacked high by the fireplace, on the chairs, on the floor.

All my old fiction books are on the bedroom bookshelves and covered with so much dust I am now afraid to touch them for fear of asphyxiation.

A further word about this villain "Dust;" He never leaves–Dust only disappears in self defense when I, with great determination, dust the room but he's only in hiding, because, by the end of the day, he quits his hiding place and is jeering at me again from all the furniture surfaces. I get no respect from Dust. No matter how hard I try. I never win our battles.

I know the source of all that fine silt that covers everything. It's our dogs; four very large, very shaggy, virtually non-shedding dogs, each of which is a perfect dust mop. My problem is, instead of shaking out their collected dust *outside,* they bring it in with themselves and shake it out *inside*. Hence my almost insoluble problem, for I am not getting rid of the dogs, just to have an immaculate house. Besides, I realize now, looking round, it's not just the dust. It's my books, my clutter, *and* the dust.

So, I decide, I will play a game. For the next hour I will work with a detective to find the source of my household chagrin. Having just had my lunch, I've decided that, before I start I'll take a few postprandial minutes whilst my food settles (I bet my stomach is also cluttered at the moment) and think about what sort of detective I want. I immediately realize, even before getting to my detective, one of the traits I have that could be contributing to my problem, is I am an *exceptional* procrastinator....

Oh well–being a writer, I have an inherent need to create a character, one I can relate to, for my detective, so join me as I create her:

She owns her own detective agency, which she runs by herself, as she can't afford an assistant. She's tall, young, and, of course, absolutely gorgeous (I'm short, bordering on old, and if I ever *was* gorgeous, it was fleeting and probably only by candlelight) the name of her agency is "Tumbleweeds." Very apropos, don't you think?

She has just been hired, by this short, bordering-on-old writer, who wants her to find out the source of her cluttered discontent.

She too has a dog, an English Bull-dog named Eugene. He sheds copiously and, although he's fairly well behaved, he does snore. All totally irrelevant, as he won't appear again in this story, but you have to admit, it does add depth.

So my detective is now standing in the middle of my living room surrounded by madly barking and wildly leaping, dogs.... NO. Wait! - This is a *story*. In real life the dogs would be barking, leaping all over the place and creating even more dust but let's calm it down a bit–she has been greeted by four well behaved dogs, who have now gone back to sleep. The detective - hang on a minute... This tall gorgeous detective has to have a name. Let me think.... GOT IT. She's Cynthia ("My friends call me Cyn") Althorp, Private Investigator. As we are not friends but just acquaintances (after all we've only just met) we'll call her Cynthia.

I explain my dust problems to Cynthia as she pulls out a pair of those latex rubber gloves the TV characters in CSI keep putting on and runs one finger along the top of the coffee table, dusted in her honor that very morning. She holds up one very dusty finger and looks at me. "Evidence," she says.

Standing beside her I look at the scene with fresh eyes and try to see what she sees.

The first thing I realize, if you ignore the dust, is that the room really doesn't look too bad. There is a comfy leather couch catty-cornered across the room. It is decorated with a large black dog, snoring softly. Close by is a big easy chair in black and white adorned by another sleeping dog.

There is a rather nice small oriental rug on the floor in an opposite corner with a round table, big enough for two, and a charming English garden bench to one side of it. Under the table are two more dogs stretched out asleep. There are a lot of books, in fact, most surfaces are covered with them but it all looks friendly and welcoming.

Cynthia turns to look out the floor to ceiling picture windows and I turn with her and as always the view takes my breath away. The house is perched high

142

on a bank overlooking a winding river with just marshland, not houses, visible across its wide expanse. The view is the reason we bought the house.

I smile with pleasure until Cynthia walks to the window and runs another gloved finger down its surface. I pull my vision back from the view and realize that the window is covered with muddy paw prints and that dirty mist that happens when dogs breathe against windows.

I rush to explain:

"It's the squirrels. All our dogs have a high prey drive and there are two squirrels that come by daily to taunt them because they can't get out. They spend a lot of time at these windows jumping and barking..." I trail off. Those windows are really dirty–it matters not that they were washed yesterday morning. Cynthia doesn't know that.

Oh, oh-I have a problem; I just made Cynthia up and now I am treating her like she really exists and I am feeling guilty in front of her.

That's what happens when you write stories; your characters become real and start to take over. I hope she is not going to take over and then, when she gets stuck, turn to me and say: "Well? It's your story – what do you want me to do now?" and I will have to bail her out...

Cynthia interrupts my train of thought.

"Why don't you let me look around on my own and I will ask questions as I need to"

I nod and, trailing behind her as she moves through the house, she asks the occasional question, "How often do you clean?" My reply of, "Obviously not enough," doesn't even raise a smile. I'm worried now that I've created a humorless character. And I am beginning to have serious doubts about this experiment.

143

I comfort myself with the thought that she can't discuss what she sees with anyone else and she'll be gone soon.

"Can I speak with your husband please? I have a few questions I would like to ask him."

I realize that this has gone far enough!

"No Cynthia I don't think so. Let's just go over what you've got and you give me your findings. I'll take it from there."

"Well, OK. That's certainly your choice but input from your husband would help confirm my conclusions."

"Thanks for being so thorough but, as I created you, I am sure you will have what I need to fix this." And I gesture around the room.

She smiles at me. A dazzling smile, and I reluctantly smile in return.

"Don't worry," she says, "It's not really bad. You have a very nice house."

"So what's the verdict?" I ask.

"Well, the real solution to your problem is, as you already know, to get rid of the dogs–which you don't intend to do. I know!" She says, as I open my mouth to protest, "You love them and they are staying."

I nod vigorously.

"Can you afford a cleaning service?"

I shake my head "No," equally vigorously.

"Well then. I think you already know your solution."

I look at her enquiringly. "And that is?"

She grins at me

"Live with it!"

And that's when I realize, despite my earlier misgivings; I have created the perfect character.

"Thank You Cyn!" I say warmly, as I escort her to the door.

"Can I get your business card before you leave? I may need your help in the future."

SQUEEZE PLAY

By: Peggy Jaegly

His fingers clutched around her white neck. His hands. But as if someone else's. He crushed her flesh tighter. Her nails clawed at his gloves, then sleeves. He barely heard her frantic, struggling gasps. Her windpipe snapped underneath his thumbs. "Huh," he thought, "This is easy. Just like squeezing a football."

Detective Blaise Morgan dropped the cloth over Katie Kendall's body. "Strangled," he muttered. "But no struggle," he added, noting the neat room. "She knew her killer. Who found her?"

"Her son, Christopher," an officer replied, "and his friend, Tom Harris."

"How old are they?"

"Both fifteen. They attend the school where Ms. Kendall taught."

"I'll talk to them." The detective sighed. When it came to youth, he used to only have to worry about kids sneaking beers, but now, with all the violence on television and video games, more and more he heard of young men and women committing murder. He wondered every day if his own daughter was safe in the high school.

"We found this on the floor," the officer said.

Morgan glanced at the Oakland High School Sports jacket. Both sleeves were ripped near the cuffs. "Bag it. Tag it." He glanced over to the teens sitting on the sofa. Christopher was pale and shaking. His friend sat silently near him. Morgan nodded in their direction and asked the Sergeant, "Have they admitted anything?"

"Nope."

"Where's her husband?"

"Out of state. Divorced six months. We're trying to locate him now."

"Call the principal. Find out what grades the boys are getting and who might want the teacher dead. Meanwhile, take them to the station for statements." The detective watched the EMTs zip up the body bag. "Call Social Services, the son can't return here until we notify his father."

"Christopher, I'm Detective Blaise Morgan," he said as he entered the interrogation room. "Thirsty?" he set a canned soda on the table. He studied the boy who hung his head low and didn't establish eye contact. His hair was short and tousled but his clothes were neat, middle class. "Do you go by Chris?" At the boy's nod, he continued." I'm sorry about your mom. Can you tell me what happened?"

"Tom and I got home after football practice. I f-f-found my m-m-mom lying on the floor by the couch. I tried to wake her up, but . . . she d-d-didn't wake up." The boy sobbed. He dipped his head and furiously wiped his tears.

"Did you have a fight today with your mom?"

"No!" Chris turned his head and stared blankly out the window.

148

"What can you tell me about this?" Morgan held up a large, clear evidence bag containing a sports jacket. The boy visibly shuddered.

"That's mine. Give it back!"

"And yet the sleeves are ripped," Morgan commented.

"I don't know why. My mom wouldn't let me wear it today."

"Why?"

"She wanted to take some stupid photo of me wearing it to send to my dad. But she was out of film. She didn't want me get it dirty until she got a picture."

"So you argued?"

"Yes. But I didn't kill her!"

"She did pick up the film today," Morgan said. "Her shopping bag was on the hall table."

"Can I have my jacket back now?"

"It's ripped."

"I don't care. I want it back!"

"Right now it's evidence. We need to keep it awhile and run some tests on it."

Morgan answered the insistent ring of his cell phone. He listened in silence but watched the teenager's sullen expression. Chris shrank under his gaze. "Got it, thanks." Snapping his phone shut, he continued. "I understand your dad is out of town. We're trying to reach him. Is there somebody you'd like to call?"

Chris nodded. "My coach."

Morgan nodded to an officer nearby. "Let him call. Have the coach meet us here."

"Here? Why?" the boy's voice tensed into a higher octave. "I want to go home. I mean...somewhere."

149

"You can't go to your house right now," the detective explained. "We are still processing it. I can't have people traipsing over the crime scene. Is there anything you want to tell me?"

"Like what?" Chris challenged. "I already told you. I didn't kill her. I just found her." He broke down in sobs. The detective excused himself, making his way to the room where Tom waited.

After Morgan listened to Tom recount a similar story about discovering the body, he casually commented, "Nice jacket."

"We just got 'em."

"Was Ms. Kendall one of your teachers?"

"Yeah. For English."

"I heard you were temporarily suspended from the team today."

"How'd you —" Tom pursed his lips and shrugged his shoulders.

"Your grades slipped and Ms. Kendall pulled the plug on you. Did you and Chris go to Ms. Kendall's house tonight to even the score?"

"No. It wasn't like that!"

"I hope not. But just in case, we're going to call your parents and have them meet us here."

"They're going to kill me!"

"We won't let that happen," Morgan assured him.

Half an hour later, two men approached Morgan's desk. "Coach Jackson, thanks for coming," said the detective, extending his hand. "I recognize you from the sports page. You've had a phenomenal winning career."

The coach shook his hand and introduced his companion, "This is my friend and attorney, Lawrence Stein."

"Where's Chris and Tom?" the lawyer asked.

Morgan pointed.

"I've been retained by Mr. Jackson," Stein explained. "You are not to interrogate the boys unless I'm present. I want to speak with them now."

"Spencer!" Morgan shouted. "Boys are lawyered up. Show Mr. Stein where to go."

Morgan turned back to the coach. "What made you bring a lawyer? We haven't charged the boys with anything."

"I heard you were a hard ass. Chris panicked. When he called me, he said you accused him of killing his mother." The Coach's jaw hardened as he stared in the detective's face. "They're two of my star players."

Morgan studied Coach Jackson from head to toe. "Nice jacket. We could almost have a fashion show."

Jackson held out his arms in front of him to admire the jacket, exposing smooth wrists. "These just came in. They're nice," he said with pride. "It took a year of fund raisers to outfit all of our teams."

"What do you know about the boys' relationships with Ms. Kendall?"

"Aw, they're good kids. No trouble."

"You have a critical game on Friday. Tom, your best running back, was sidelined by Ms. Kendall. Were you upset?"

He paused before answering, "Disappointed," and with a smirk he added, "but we always tell the team their studies come first."

"Uh huh. And your personal relationship with her?"

151

"We're colleagues."

"Did you date?"

"No, we hardly saw each other."

"Not even during lunch?"

"We're assigned hall duty on opposite sides."

"And yet the principal overheard a heated discussion between you two today."

"Mere words, detective. I was pleading Tom's case but Katie was a hard-head. . . , firm in her resolve to flunk him in English."

"The assistant principal says Ms. Kendall confided to her that you were interested in more than school matters."

"Detective." Mr. Stein summoned as he strode down the hallway. "A word with you please."

Morgan sequestered himself with the attorney in a nearby office. Through the window, he watched Coach Jackson pacing the corridor.

"Neither boy killed Mrs. Kendall," Stein claimed. " I think we can find the murderer quickly if we assemble the entire sports teams or anyone who received the new Oakland jackets. To prove it, my client Chris needs immunity for what would be a misdemeanor since he's a minor."

Morgan contemplated the fidgety coach for a moment. "We may not have to assemble the entire team. Okay, I'll clear it with the D.A. Chris has immunity. What went down?"

"Chris confided in me that he purposefully took out a few stitches in the bottom of his left jacket pocket to hide a few un-prescribed steroid pills in the lining of his jacket. No intention of distributing."

Morgan phoned the lab. As he hung up, he responded to the attorney, "No tear in either pocket."

Opening the door, he requested, "Coach Jackson, would you join us please?"

"Are you releasing the boys?" said the coach, grinning while he gave a friendly slap on his attorney's shoulder.

"Soon," Morgan promised him. "I need you to do one thing."

"Name it."

"Snap your jacket shut."

"What?"

"Humor me."

"Fine." The coach tugged each side of the jacket and snapped it shut.

"Seems a bit snug to me." he turned to the attorney. "Does it to you?"

"Let's see," Morgan pulled up the coach's arms, as if he were a doll with moveable parts. The jacket strained. Morgan shoved his hand into the left pocket. "Hm, a new jacket and it already has a tear." Withdrawing his hand and patting the side of the jacket, he felt three round bulges near the bottom seam.

"You can't search me," the coach protested.

"Probable cause," Morgan and Stein answered in unison.

"Coach William Jackson, you're under arrest for the murder of Katie Kendall." After Morgan recited the Miranda rights, he added, "You're a low life for trying to pin a murder on a kid. When you knew Chris wouldn't be home, you went to Ms. Kendall's home to change her mind. She refused. Sweet-talking didn't work either. She rejected you and you killed her. But you didn't count on her ripping your jacket. Chris must have complained about his mother to you, so you knew his jacket was in the house and you switched them. Our lab will find the DNA evidence to support this, so no use in denying it."

Coach Jackson turned to his attorney. "Larry?"

"Forget it. Find someone else." Lawrence Stein snapped his briefcase shut and headed down the corridor to the boys.

Morgan raised his eyebrows. "You're out of the game, Coach. You ought to know squeeze plays belong in baseball, not football."

MOWING TO A DIFFERENT DRUMMER

By: Linda Garman Weimer

Oh, the yearning for simpler times! It's the urge that spurs us to bake bread at home, or to mend a favorite garment by taking a few stitches by hand. Such a wish led me, a first-time owner of a lawn, to buy a non-powered, push-only lawnmower– technically known as a reel mower. After all, I only have a quarter acre, and that plot is reduced by some vinca plants headed toward a groundcover.

Ah –the smell of fresh-cut grass without the odor of gasoline fumes. Hmmm - the quiet that would surround me as I rolled the simple device across the turf. The blades made a nifty whisk-whisk sound in the store, like a drummer playing his brushes.

Yes! There were going to be many mornings of leisurely exercise and communion with nature.

But I had assumed one thing would carry over from nasty, smelly modern methods. I assumed the grass would still be cut.

Well, there was the rub. My lawn looked like the straggly beard of a 15-year-old boy more than a finished mowing job. The whiskers were the many uncut strands of crabgrass, bugle weeds, wild onions and other weeds that take a bump of the reel mower and, like the old commercials said, kept on tickin.'

With my fantasy failing, I went for help. After the expert at my local hardware store vigorously hand-cranked the reel mower to sharpen its blades, as called for in the directions, I noted a little improvement. But mainly the improvement came from backing up the mower and attacking stubborn tufts from a different direction. And then from another different direction. After four hours of work, I still have not made my way around the entire yard.

I got some advice from my brother, a home-landscaper whose lawn always looks immaculate. "That's why modern mowers have rotary blades," he said. "The reel mower cuts only from one angle. Rotary blades cut from the full 360 degrees in a single pass," he pointed out.

"Don't you remember Dad's old reel mower? How he had to keep backing up to cut at a different angle?" I didn't remember.

"That's why he bought a power rotary mower as soon as possible," brother said.

I discussed the machine's poor performance with some friends. "Leisurely exercise" is a delusion, they said. "You have to almost run with it, to build up enough force in the blades," said one person with reel-mower experience.

With bad joints, I can't see that happening. And, there are still those side benefits of–let's call it *trimming* my lawn.

I *do* smell the fresh fragrance of cut grass, see the birds caper about, and most surprisingly, have learned that adjusting my standards to allow for more pleasure and less perfection is not so bad.

However, I have some neighbors. Most of them use riding mowers, which knock off their entire properties in under an hour. The neighbors also have much neater lawns than mine. No one has actually said anything to me yet. But then, the bugleweeds are still only nine inches tall.

Maybe I can work out a truce with a paid grass-cutter. He can mow most of the lawn, leaving me just the square foot around each vinca.

LONGFELLOW
By: Nancy Hartman

Longfellow was a man of great sentiments and affections. Fellow writer Nathaniel Hawthorne (1804-1864) and abolitionist Senator Charles Sumner (1811-1874) were his closest and lifelong friends.

Although Hawthorne and Longfellow went through Bowdoin College together, graduating in 1825, they did not see or communicate with one another for twelve years. In 1837 Hawthorne published "Twice-told Tales" and sent a copy of it to Longfellow in the hope that he would review it: *"I should like to flatter myself that these tales would repay you some part of the pleasure which I have derived from your own."* Almost immediately, Longfellow sent Hawthorne a long and warm reply, studded with compliments.

An ailing Hawthorne died in his sleep in 1864. Longfellow was one of the pallbearers. He wrote the poem "May 19, 1846": *"How beautiful it was, that one bright day in the long week of rain! Though all its splendor could not chase away the omnipresent pain. I was as one who wanders in a trance, unconscious of his road. For the one face I looked for was not there; the one low voice was mute; only an unseen presence filled the air and baffled my pursuit. There in seclusion and remote from men the wizard hand lies cold, which at its topmost speed let fall the pen, and left the tale half told."*

Sumner was Longfellow's most frequent visitor to the Longfellow house for almost 35 years. When Sumner died in 1874, Longfellow wrote a poem in his memory. *"Alike are life and death when life in death survives, and the uninterrupted breath inspires a thousand lives. When a star quenched on high for ages would its light, still travelling downward from the sky, shine on our mortal sight, so when a great man dies, for years beyond our ken, the light he leaves behind him lies upon the paths of men."*

He married his first wife, Mary Potter, in 1831. She died in 1835 several weeks after a miscarriage. She was 22. *"One thought occupies me night and day. She is dead! All day I am weary and sad."* He wrote the poem "Footsteps of Angels" about her. *"With a slow and noiseless footstep comes that messenger divine; takes the vacant chair beside me, lays her gentle hand in mine. And she sits and gazes at me with those deep and tender eyes, like the stars, so still and saint-like, looking downward from the skies."*

He married his second wife Frances Appleton in 1843. She was the daughter of a wealthy Boston industrialist. *"Victory hangs doubtful. The lady says she will not. I say she shall!"* He courted her for seven years. During that time he was so afraid he might lose her that he had periods of neurotic depression with moments of panic, and he took a six-month leave from his professorship at Harvard to attend a German spa at a Benedictine Convent. At last, she said yes.

Learning of this by her letter, he was too excited to take a carriage and instead walked 90 minutes to her house. Her father bought the "Craigie House" in Cambridge as a wedding present for them. The house had been the headquarters of General Washington during the Revolutionary War. *"Oh, my beloved! My sweet Hesperus! My morning and evening star of love!"*

He once attended a ball without her: *"The lights seemed dimmer, the music sadder, the flowers fewer, and the women less fair."* They had five children, including three daughters.

"Between the dark and the daylight, when the night is beginning to lower, comes a pause in the day's occupations that is known as the Children's Hour."

So begins one of the most famous poems in English literature, written by the poet laureate of his day in 1860.

"From my study I see in the lamplight, descending the broad hall stair, grave Alice and laughing Allegra and Edith with golden hair.

A whisper, and then a silence: yet I know by their merry eyes they are plotting and planning together to take me by surprise.

I have you fast in my fortress and will not let you depart, but will put you down in the dungeon in the round-tower of my heart.

And there I will keep you forever, yes, forever and a day, 'til the walls shall crumble to ruin and moulder in dust away!"

Frances died in 1861 after sustaining severe burns when her dress caught on fire from a fireplace ember. Longfellow, who had been in another room napping, raced to her side to help her put out the fire. She died of her burns the next morning. Longfellow was burned badly enough that he could not attend her funeral. He thereafter grew a beard to hide his facial scars. He never fully recovered from her death. He occasionally resorted to opium and ether to deal with it. He was afraid he would go mad and begged to not be taken to an asylum, noting that he was inwardly bleeding to death.

In 1879, prompted by sight of a mountain view, he wrote "Cross of Snow." It was not published in his lifetime. *"In the long sleepless watches of the night a gentle face – the face of one long dead – looks at me from the wall, where round its head the night-lamp casts a halo of pale light. The sun, defying in its deep ravines, displays a cross of snow upon its side. Such is the cross I wear these eighteen years, through all the changing scenes and seasons, changeless since the day she died."*

He died in 1882 and is buried in Cambridge, Massachusetts with both of his wives.

Longfellow was a man of great passions and sentiments. Longfellow was a man in love.

Longfellow was born in 1807 in a section of Maine that was then part of Massachusetts. He was the second of eight children.

Longfellow was named after his mother's brother, Henry Wadsworth, a Navy lieutenant who died at the Battle of Tripoli. His maternal grandfather was a general in the Revolutionary War, his uncle was a trustee of Bowdoin College, and his father was a lawyer.

He was known as a very serious student. His mother encouraged his enthusiasm for reading and learning. He published his first poem at the age of 13. Upon his graduation from Bowdoin College, he wrote, *"I most eagerly aspire after full eminence in literature; my whole soul burns most ardently after it. I believe that if I can ever rise in the world it must be by the exercise of my talents in the wide field of literature."* He became a professor of literature at Bowdoin; later at Harvard.

His literary income increased substantially from 1850 to 1870. In 1850 he was making about $250 a month. By 1860 it was about $1,900 a month. By 1870 he was making $48,000 a year.

GASOLINE ALLEY

By: Larry Samuels

The rubber hose clanged the service bell twice –
someone had driven over it completely up to the first gas
pump. "I'll get it," Sal said to Slim Willy sitting next to
him.

Sal got up from the chair that was set on a small
curb just outside of the gas station office, tugged at the
rag sticking out of the back pocket of his green uniform
pants and walked directly to the driver's side of the red
and white four-door '57 Plymouth Plaza. It was 1969.

The guy driving it said, "Fill it up, please,
regular." Sometimes they said please, sometimes they
didn't. This wasn't much of a concern to Sal. He would
pump gas for them whether they asked nicely or not. He
walked around past the back of the car, opened the fuel
door on the side panel, reached for the hose nozzle, lifted
it from its cradle, pulled up on it to start the pump,
placed the nozzle in the fuel funnel, squeezed the handle
and flipped the holder to the last ridge to keep it
pumping. It would click off when the tank was nearly
full.

He took the squeegee from the bucket of water at
the end of the fueling island and sponged the windshield
wet, then cleaned it off with the rubber blade. "Check
your oil?' he said to the driver. "Yeah, sure," he
answered. Sal placed the squeegee back in the bucket,

eyeballed the spinning dials to see where he thought he might be in closing in on the fill-up, then reached under the front edge of the hood to pop it open. As the hood was held open by hydraulic arms, he pulled the oil dipstick out, wiped it with his rag, bottomed it back in, pulled it out again and could see from the glistening oil film that the level was within range, and not too dirty. The fuel pump clicked off.

"Oil's good," he said out loud. He walked over to the pump and squeezed the handle again to top off the tank at what was usually a dead-on even-dollar amount, or at a five or ten-cent increment. He didn't often miss.

"That'll be $7.50," he said. It was about twelve gallons. The driver pulled out his wallet and handed Sal a five and three dollar bills. "Keep the change, buddy," he said. That was a treat – sometimes they tipped, mostly not. And for fifty-cents this time, not too bad. Usually it would be a quarter, if anything. "Thanks, pal," Sal answered. The guy started the car and drove out of the station, clanging over the next hose, into a relatively light traffic pattern. It was just past 10:00 p.m. One more hour, Sal thought, then I'm out of here.

He walked back to his chair and sat down, but didn't feel a need to say anything to Slim Willy, the other guy on this shift. Willy was a friendly, family man, a nice guy to work with, who knew the score. He was shorter than Sal, wiry, and still spoke with a southern drawl carried from his being born and raised in Georgia.

Sal and he got along well – Sal got along with most everyone. Some nights he worked with Willy, some nights with his other partner, Big Bill, an affable gentleman, way street smart – he had a long, dark scar across the back of his neck, the remains of a long-ago card game that had gone very wrong. Bill was a gigantic,

164

thick man, standing well over 6'-5" and strong, capable of effortlessly lifting heavy wheels onto the pneumatic machine to break down tires from rims to fix flats.

Sal was slightly feeling the strain of walking back and forth from this evening's work. At 5'-9", stocky, with thick curly black hair, brown eyes and a clean-shaven face, he could work for long periods of time, but was feeling just a little tired this night.

He had been working at this service station on Coney Island Avenue in Brooklyn, New York for about a year and a half. He came in at 5:00 p.m. and worked until he closed up at 11:00 p.m., five nights a week. At least he didn't have to work on the weekends – that was great. Willy and Bill shared alternate weekends with two other employees that Sal would sometimes run into.

This weeknight job was actually after school. Sal was attending a local community college, majoring in the preliminary courses required for a two-year Liberal Arts degree. He really didn't have much direction after being graduated from high school two years before.

He was basically attending college to avoid the military draft, with the prospect of being shipped directly to Vietnam if he did get drafted.

He was fortunate to be working these hours. He could still attend school and he was making money. At the hourly rate of $1.75, he was making $.50 per hour above the current minimum wage. He was always in cigarette money, could buy gas for his car and could entertain dates. He was living at home with his parents, two sisters and a brother and had secured a student loan to pay for his tuition.

He had turned eighteen after high school and had registered for the draft. He held a 2-S deferment classification as a college student, however that would change to 1-A if he left school. It was pretty elitist to provide draft deferments for college students, but that was the contemporary landscape. Deferments were also being provided for teachers – a more noble enterprise. Some guys were also getting draft deferments for essential work – hospital power plants, like that.

Once his classification changed, it could likely be just a matter of time before he would be drafted into the Army to serve in Vietnam. Not a good situation. He had lost a Marine cousin to the war, having been killed during the Tet Offensive a year before, in 1968 at Khe Sanh, the base located in the district capital of Quang Tri province. It was overwhelming, a horrifying time for the family.

The entire family had been devastated and was now facing the possibility of losing another member, if Sal went over. His leaving school, if he did, would start the clock on his induction. It wasn't a certainty that he would go straight to Vietnam, but it was a very distinct possibility.

Sal wasn't that gung-ho about putting himself in that situation of being in the military in order to defend his country. His patriotism was indistinct and not a priority for him. There was no tradition in his family of especially noteworthy military service, just the obligatory World War II involvement experienced by his father and several uncles, and the death of his cousin.

It didn't seem to him that he needed to be in the direct line of fire to have to live up to any ideal or to prove anything to anyone. Just by completing a standard regulation stint in the military would suffice for his own personal satisfaction, and would be in conformance with what he believed to be customary behavior within his socio-economic class.

He wasn't overly intellectual about all of this, however. As far as military service, he wasn't against it at all, even in these dangerous times during the war of ground combat and extreme negativity towards the military – and extreme support. These were the days of "Hawks" and "Doves," of the philosophy, "America, Love It, or Leave It." He could see that there were benefits to having military training and experience. It would mean being able to take advantage of the GI Bill for education and of a Veteran's Administration Home Loan – he could see all that. His father had gone to school after WW II and had used his VA loan to buy their first house. There were positive aspects of military service, however, one had to live through the experience to make that work.

Although he could see the benefits, he only wanted to limit the extent of catastrophic circumstances that he might encounter. While military service seemed to be honorable, it certainly didn't have to include direct combat in Vietnam.

The purpose of the war in Vietnam was fairly obscure to him. It wasn't talked about at all in any of his classes throughout junior high school or high school during the mid-to-late sixties – not that he had experienced these academic exercises.

They did learn about world history in school – European history, that is, and not too much ever about Asia or Africa, of which he didn't remember learning a whole lot about that area of the world, except for the part about European colonization.

Because the war was all around him, he did think that he might eventually be very involved in it. He wasn't particularly affected, however, by the major protests against the war going on at the time, almost all of which seemed to be by college students.

Vietnam Veterans themselves, however, were also starting to make statements against the war. His politics, though, were not in alignment with any movement. None of his friends were talking about the war, only about how they were hoping to avoid being drafted.

During those times when the war was on, job candidates were being asked by prospective employers, during interviews, just what was their draft status. Companies weren't too keen on hiring and then training people who would potentially have to go into the military.

It was difficult for males of draft age who had some vision of their career paths to be able to focus on their plans, with the possible disruption of their lives beckoning them in the near future. It was a very real dilemma in relation to general employment, not to mention the obvious doubts about actual survival, or if one would physically or mentally remain whole, if one went into combat.

This kind of job analysis didn't apply to Sal's employment as a gas station attendant while still in school. He hadn't been asked about his draft status when he was hired to pump gas. His uncle had worked at this gas station about a year before Sal and the owner had been satisfied that he had vouched for Sal as an honest, hard-working man. He was safe in school and at the station for the time being. The looming specter of Vietnam was still in the future, as long as he stayed in school. Slim Willy and Big Bill were way past draft age, both black men in their forties and Army veterans of World War II. Sal was much younger and white. They all got along famously – Sal was interested to hear about their service during the war, although they didn't talk about it much.

As far as his getting along in this racially mixed environment in 1968, he had been raised in a very progressive and tolerant household and had always been hustling work since his early teens with a variety of nationalities. Not that he was actively involved in any way with the Civil Rights movement, but he couldn't understand the appalling culture of racism in the country, and did experience a terrible and deep sense of loss that spring when he heard over the radio that Dr. Martin Luther King, Jr. had been assassinated in Memphis, Tennessee. He knew the country would never be the same.

It wasn't too busy during the next hour at work. A few cars came in, no flat tires to fix, and he and Willy shared pumping gas. About 10:45 p.m., Sal started to close up. He took a clipboard with a chart from its hook on a wall in the office and read the meters on the fuel pumps.

He went into the garage area and to the electrical panel, shutting down the circuit breakers for the pumps and the floodlights.

He counted the money in the cash register, placed the few credit card charge slips together and placed all of that in an empty plastic juice pitcher. He tucked the pitcher into a space on one of the shelves in the supply closet in the back of the office. It was Frank's idea, the station owner, who thought keeping the night receipts casually like that in the shop was a lot safer than having Sal as the night manager walk it to the bank depository.

Frank would be coming in the next morning to check Sal's accounting and would make whatever bank deposit he needed to make. Frank trusted Sal and he really had a lot of responsibility at his age.

Sal and Willy changed out of their coverall uniforms into street clothes. Sal shut out the office lights and locked the door. They said goodnight to each other and Willy jumped in to his 1963 four-door Pontiac Bonneville Safari station wagon. Not a particularly special vehicle, but for Willy and his wife and four children it was good transportation. The trouble was that Willy's car usually had a few cockroaches in it – the result of his bringing various bags full of clothes and other items to the car from his house, which also had cockroaches. These transports, and the habit that Willy had of always eating in his car – this kept the cockroaches happy.

Now it was time for Sal to grab a bite to eat. This section of Coney Island Avenue, and most of the rest of it, from Bartel-Pritchard Square at the northern entrance of Prospect Park, about two miles away, and to the south, at Brighton Beach Avenue on the edge of Coney Island, almost exclusively contained other gas stations at approximately two block intervals.

Crammed in between the stations were car repair shops, used car lots, new car dealerships, tire shops, car washes, auto glass replacement shops, car sound system installation shops, foreign and domestic auto parts stores, cab companies and car rental companies – this was gasoline alley.

The nearest places to eat were about a half-mile down the avenue. It was either at "George's," a coffee shop and luncheonette, or the almost-famous "Big Daddy's," a "Nathan's" type hot dog, hamburger, French fries and beer joint, with a parking lot.

Sal got into his car, a steel gray '61 Chevrolet Bel Air, two-door sedan. Big eight cylinders, 283 cubic inch engine, weighed just under 3,500 pounds: a really great automobile. Although it sold for about $2,600 new in 1961, now these eight years later he had scraped together the $525 he had paid for it used, from his savings while working all during high school, helping his father run the house after his mother died. He had delivered dry cleaning for a neighborhood store after school and managed the Laundromat next door to that for three nights during the week and on weekends. He had always worked, delivering orders for the local butcher shop, at one of the neighborhood grocery stores packing orders, always had a few dollars in his pocket.

Being employed at the gas station gave him the opportunity to work on his Chevrolet as needed – not that it needed a lot of work at this time, even though it had almost 100,000 miles on it, but he could keep it

171

tuned up, changing spark plugs, points, condenser, oil and filter, keeping the engine timed, replacing brakes, like that. It was good to be on gasoline alley.

He drove to "Big Daddy's." Parking, then going to the counter, he ordered a hamburger, French fries and a soda. He sat at one of the outdoor tables, ate, then smoked a cigarette. It was getting late and he had an early class the next morning. Although he sometimes almost slept through the early ones, he wasn't doing too badly at school, maintaining about a B average. He just needed to stick it out until he could figure out what he was going to do about his future.

Without a career direction, he wasn't really satisfied staying there in school, but wasn't exactly ready yet to enlist in the Navy, an option that he had been considering. Joining up would end the uncertainty of the draft.

That next night, Sal was back at work, pumping gas, checking oil, checking water, cleaning windshields, basically relaxed and not unhappy. He was working with Bill tonight. The conversation between them was lively and full of stories. Bill liked to talk and Sal could keep up with him.

About 9:00 p.m., a dark blue '65 Mustang fastback with white-wall tires pulled in. Sitting there behind the steering wheel was a dark-haired woman wearing a Tee shirt and a cut-off dungaree jacket. The rock music from her radio was turned up loud. She turned it off and shut down the engine. To Sal, she looked a few years older than him.

Sal walked over, leaned down to her face, looked directly into her blue eyes and said, "Can I help you, miss?"

She looked up at him for a moment, looking down at her, and said, "I need a fill-up, high test. Then I need you to check my front." Sal didn't blink – for some reason she had clearly found an immediate connection just by looking at him.

"Sure, I can take care of that for you." He was only slightly thinking about pumping gas. He was, however, thinking about filling her tank, so to speak. He went over to the pump, opened the fuel door at the rear of the car and started putting gas in. He walked to the front of her car, smiling into the windshield. She smiled back. He lifted the hood and checked the fluids. Oil, radiator, power steering and brake fluids were fine. He would have to check the transmission after she started the car again, if he would get to that. He didn't think that he would, however. The pump clicked off. He was going to make sure he clicked back on with her.

He stopped the pump, walked around to her side, leaned down and said, "It came to $5.00. By the way, nice ride you've got, nice paint color, great engine, that 289 V-8. I know you can move pretty fast in this car. Anything else I can do for you?".

He liked what he saw. His wheels were spinning fast into what he hoped would be the very near future.

"Well, I don't need anything else right now," she said. "I have to be somewhere else tonight, soon. You like this car? So do I, it fits me really well, like a glove. I like things that have a nice fit."

To Sal, there was no mistaking what she was talking about. Although Sal was no slouch when it came to dating and sexual contact, this exchange was going as

173

fast as that Mustang of hers and his Chevy could go. They were racing together at top speed.

"I've been driving this car since last year when I bought it. Let me get money out of my handbag." She stretched over to the passenger side, real slow. He watched as her jeans inched down a little over her shapely behind. He was impressed.

She handed him a ten-dollar bill. "You keep the change, honey," she said. "I'm going to start gassing up here from now on."

"Fine by me, I'm here every weeknight, but I'm free on the weekends. Thanks, that's a really nice tip."

"It's worth it for good service. I'll be back real soon, when I need more service."

"Sure. My name's Sal, what's yours?".

"I'm Jane. Nice to meet you, Sal. Thanks for the gas."

"No, thank you for your gift – you're now one of my best customers, and the nicest looking.".

She smiled, started the car and stepped hard on the accelerator, burning a little rubber as she pulled out. He watched as she pulled out of the station and onto the street. Would she be back the next night? He certainly hoped so, but then he had the expectation that she would be there. It was an electric meeting. Hard to explain, just one look like that, but it happened sometimes, especially in 1969.

Bill said, "Hey boy, what was that all about? Looked like you were checking out more than her oil."

"Oh, yeah, something going on there. Nice looking car, nice looking driver – I hope I'll be filling her up with something real soon."

Bill laughed. "Good luck, buddy, fine young thing there in that fine car. Thinking about that, I think I'll see my girlfriend tonight."

"You take it easy, Bill, don't strain your old self."

Bill laughed even harder. "Don't worry about me, kid, I can handle it. Hope you can."

Sal closed the station at 11:00 p.m. He would be working with Bill the next night as well. Bill drove off in his car, a throaty-sounding 1960, two-door Ford Galaxy, with reflectors on the mud flaps behind the rear wheels. Instead of "Big Daddy's" Sal hit the coffee shop for a bacon, lettuce and tomato sandwich on rye toast, with a cup of coffee. Then he went home to wait until tomorrow.

It was about 10:00 p.m. the next night. Sal had not had any classes that day. He was sitting in his chair outside of the office with Bill. The blue Mustang pulled in alongside the pump island. Sal got up and walked over to greet her.

"Hi, Jane, how's it going?"

"I'm fine, you OK?"

"Yeah, I'm good. What can I get for you?"

"Nothing here, I don't need any gas since yesterday. But there's something you can help me with at my house." She was looking right at him and he was looking right back at her.

"Happy to oblige. You're just in time. Let me close up here and change my clothes, I'll be right with you."

"Why don't you just close and you can change at my house."

Even this was fast for Sal. "Sure, I'll be right with you. Why don't you just pull over to the other side

175

of this island?" She moved the car away from the pumps and left the motor running.

Bill said brightly, "I guess I know what you're doing tonight."

"As soon as we get out of here, looks like my ship has come in," Sal answered easily.

He took the readings, counted out, put the money away and grabbed his change of clothes. Bill said, "So long, see you sometime," and left the shop. Sal shut the lights and locked the door. Although somewhat distracted, his concentration on what needed to be done at the station was not debatable.

Sal opened the passenger side door of her car and got in. "My car is parked on the street around the corner," he said.

"It'll keep until tomorrow," she said. "I don't live too far from here."

"I'm all yours," he answered.

"Yes, you are," she said.

They drove north on the avenue for about five minutes, past the south entrance to Prospect Park, then a few blocks further. She parked on the street near a three-story brownstone apartment building. This section of Coney Island Avenue was all residential, with only the occasional grocery store or pizza parlor facing the park.

They walked to the building entrance, not talking. She was several inches shorter than him. She was wearing black slacks, sneakers and a tee shirt, with her dungaree jacket. Although he had partially seen what she looked like in her car, the streetlight revealed that she was indeed a good-looking woman with a trim figure. Sal was feeling pretty good.

"Here we are," she said, as she opened the apartment door on the second floor. She turned on a light in the entrance and led him to the living room. She turned on a lamp and said, "Why don't you sit down and I'll fix us a couple of drinks. I have gin – How's that?"

"Nice, thanks." He sat on the couch, a little hesitantly, considering that he was still in his work clothes, and placed his street clothes on the floor. He looked around the room. A television set, two easy chairs, a coffee table in front of the couch, an area rug and the end table with the lamp. He could see the bedroom off to the right.

She came back into the living room carrying two drinks. Handing him one, she sat down next to him.

"Cheers," she said.

"Here's to you, babe."

They took a sip, then Jane said, "You probably want to get out of those work clothes, don't you?"

"I could change," he said. "Let me go into the bathroom."

"Don't bother, Sal, why not just take them off here? I need to get out of my clothes too."

Although up to this point, even since the other night when they had first met and Jane had come on to him, they had not spoken much about anything except some small talk of how each of them was doing and some car comments, it didn't seem to matter. She, and he, just had one thing on their minds, and it was going to happen.

It was dreamy and frenzied – they helped each other to strip out of their clothes, then she lead him to the bedroom.

The next morning, Jane woke up first. She woke him.

"Sal, I need to get to work." She had told him last night that she was the bookkeeper for a small manufacturing company in downtown Brooklyn. She had been working there about three years. Before that, she had worked for a lighting supply company, also as a bookkeeper, following graduation from high school. She was twenty-seven years old.

"Sorry to see you go," he said. "It was great last night."

"Sure was, you got my motor running in high gear."

"Glad to be of service," he said.

They showered, together, then they had some coffee and buttered toast. They mostly talked about cars. They left the apartment together. Jane dropped Sal off at his car.

"Maybe I'll see you tonight," he said.

"Maybe you will," she said. "If not, I'll be around sometime."

"Looking forward to it," he said.

She didn't make it the next night. But she did come around to the station every few nights after that, during the next three months. Willy and Bill thought it was really hot, this arrangement that Sal had with this woman.

It was always the same. She would pick him up around closing time, then they would stop at an all-night coffee shop slightly north near Church Avenue for a bite to eat, then they would go to her apartment and spend the night together. They never really got past knowing each other much beyond these physical encounters. Whatever were her reasons for picking him up, it remained at just that level, a pick-up. Sal didn't mind. He wasn't really looking for something with that much commitment. He was young and independent.

He was only twenty years old and somewhat restless, with the presence of the draft and general uncertainty sharing in this relationship. He wasn't thinking about any kind of long-term commitment with a woman, not even Jane.

And then, as he thought it might end, Jane came by one night and told him that she was moving. That could have been true, or not. She wouldn't be taking him home anymore.

Nice while it lasted and all that, she said. He wasn't too upset. It had been a busy few months but there wasn't much there in the way of deep feelings on the part of either one of them. It had been convenient and anonymous. He would miss the sex, which was good, but even he needed to make some changes.

Sal stayed there at the gas station through the fall, but as the next winter approached, he made the decision to leave school, where he wasn't accomplishing much in the way of pursuing a serious education and didn't want to face the winter weather outdoors pumping gas. He had to face it.

Sure enough, once he didn't register for school, about a month later he got his 1-A draft re-classification. He didn't wait until he received the draft notice. Without much hesitation, he went to the local Navy recruiting station and was able to complete his paperwork within two weeks. He saw where he could train to be an Engineman, a mechanic for shipboard motors. Perfect. He would be starting Boot Camp in Great Lakes, Illinois, just outside of Chicago and Milwaukee, a few weeks later.

His family was concerned but supported his decision, which seemed to make sense to them – probably avoiding the worst of the fighting.

179

He gave his notice to Frank at the station and parted company with his pals, Slim Willy and Big Bill. He had goodbye sessions with family and friends and sold his car to a guy in the neighborhood, for $300.

But the last ride he took one night in that big Chevy was along the full length of gasoline alley, slowly passing every station, to have one final look for a fast, hot blue Mustang, being handled by the car's perfectly matched driver.

FORGIVING DAYS GONE BY

By: Barbara Harbeson

We humans have a funny way of collecting emotion. Some will even place into compartments and mark to designate emotion and store as if it will be needed to serve the proof of evidence at a later time.

A good example for me on this subject was that I lived with grandparents on my father's side when I was 2 ½ until 6 years old and I stored a lot of memory of things that were said and done that I recall as the discontent of my early years.

I have recently come across some pictures of that time, and I am more focused on the expressions rather than the perceived emotion. Perhaps, I had it all wrong. This clearly goes with the theorem, "you live and you learn."

One picture that truly struck me was of my Aunt. She lived with us, as did her son. He was about ten years of age at the time and as I remember, a very mean child. As we three posed for this picture, my Aunt's expression was one of pride. I remember that my Aunt made me clothes and so I was always dressed well and the expectation was that I stayed that way from dusk until dawn. Impossible! Little girls today are dressed in clothes that go anywhere, anytime and can be changed if wet or dirty, as they will go into the wash and be dry in an hour or so and that was not the case then.

And so, the emotion that went with keeping me looking like a little doll and then my cousin would throw dirt on me is now becoming a storage problem.

As I begin to go through the pictures to find that my Aunt was only being my mother for that moment in time and that she was trying to keep me looking the way people would perceive her role, I now see her point.

Older is wiser, and I am sorry that I did not appreciate her more as she was doing the best that she could in those times.

"POETRY AND HUMS"

By: Frances Reed

You reporters and interviewers are all the same.

"Why do you write?"

It's a silly question really. (I'm sorry; that sounds more rude than I meant it to) and I am sure you get all kinds of disingenuous answers: "Because I must!" "Because I can!" "If I don't write I'll die!"

Me? I feel a bit like Eeyore when he said: *"This Writing Business–Pencils and whatnot–Over rated if you ask me."*

Yes, I am trying to dodge your question because I have no clever, or clear, answer for you and, as someone who writes, I really should be able to express the *why* of: "Why I write...."

Well, the honest answer, for me, is: "I don't know why I write. I'm thrilled that I can even get anything down on paper at all; *why* I do it is the last thing on my mind!"

You see; my mind is a kaleidoscope of pictures and words, all heaped in a pile in my brain; but sometimes; when I raise that kaleidoscope to my inner eye, patterns emerge, words form and a story starts to come into view. The thing with kaleidoscope pictures though, is that once seen, they never exactly repeat themselves and in order to capture what you saw, at that moment, you write it down. If you don't do it then and there, trying to create it later results in a poor imitation of what you saw.

Understand, I'm not sifting through the pictures looking for something to use–it's not like that –it's more like the pattern starts to appear and it inserts itself in my line of vision and I see it, frozen almost whole, if you will... and I sit down at my computer in front of my blank Word page and start to type...

I'm always amazed at the results, good, bad or indifferent. Amazed, because, what was once just white space is now filled with words; words, pulled out of my brain, one by one; strung together in sentences; divided into paragraphs; punctuated (badly!) and there, there on the page, is a *story*. *My* story, *my* thoughts, *my* feelings, *my* vision and I marvel at where it came from, and how it came to be...

Do you recall, that when they first launched the Hubble telescope, the first pictures sent back to Earth were out of focus? And it wasn't until corrections were made to the Hubble's lenses that everything became sharp and clear? Writing, to me, is rather like that. My inner kaleidoscope delivers the picture that captivates me, but, until I start to type, that picture is slightly blurred and only sharpens into place on the page as I write it down.

Sometimes a story is crystal clear as I write it and any changes I make are only to eliminate repetitive words and polish the prose to a pleasing luster.

Others require re-focusing and major adjustments. Still others will never be clear and are unusable; to be abandoned like old foggy photos; the ones, where the image is dimly visible but there is nothing that can be done to bring it to the vibrant life you thought you saw and wanted it to have.

So there you have it. That's why I write: to translate the pictures I see in my mind into words that I can keep, or not, share, or not-but they are all mine.

Or, to use another metaphor: I have the huge satisfaction of someone who envisions and makes a garment, woven into whole cloth from the wool of a sheep they raised; wool they gathered, carded and spun. There can be no greater satisfaction than that,

But the vision has to come from somewhere and it's like Pooh says:

"It isn't easy-because Poetry and Hums aren't things which you get; they're things which get you. And all you can do is go where they can find you."

And if they don't find you: you don't write.

Or at least, *I* don't.

A LETTER HOME TO MINGBETISTAN, THE HAPPY KINGDOM, ABOUT BASEBALL

By: Linda Garman Weimer

Hello revered and most wonderful brother, or Kuzu Zangpo, as we would say at home:

I write in English to better your reading and to avoid translating terms that make no sense in our language. I will do my best to answer your questions about the American game of baseball. I have attended only one game, and so, even though my English is certainly excellent (you know of my many years studying with native English speakers) I should not promise that my grasp of this sport is equally expert. With a sojourn of just six months, I cannot learn all parts of American culture.

So, here you have it: From what I have seen in my 3-hour exposure to one competition, I can well comprehend why this sport has fallen in popularity. It violates all principles of good sense and pious, civilized behavior--including the wisdoms of the Buddha, Confucius, all 13 deities of the Hindu pantheon and no doubt would shock even Hammurabi despite the 5,000 years he has watched from his grave.

The most obvious offense is the overall orientation of the game, to wit: the runners on the offense ("the team at bat") must run in a counterclockwise direction, touching bags on the ground known as "bases." This assault on revealed truth insures that the players will no doubt live short and miserable lives.

As to the action: The team at bat sends a succession of men to stand at home base holding a rounded stick called a bat, while a member of the opposing team throws baseballs in his direction. But, alas, many times the thrower tries to fool the batter and throws some counterfeit creation made of who-knows-what, and the referee announces in no uncertain times that it is not a ball but a "strike."

The batter does not like such trickery, and conveys primitive anger at the announcement. (The referees evidently are chosen on the basis of superlative sense of touch.) If three such strikes are thrown to the batter, he shows his displeasure by quitting the game and reclining on a bench in the shade.

Surely these teams could use a Zen practitioner to teach them some meditative techniques with which to deal with their problems!

The hitter's goal is, apparently, to hit a ball directly to one of nine players on defense, known as "the team in the field." When this occurs, he has to run only to first base, where a defensive player has already caught a relay from his teammate. This fortunate batter can then casually run back to the bench in the shade. Such moments are the rare times in a game in which a devout citizen of Mingbetistan could find any pleasure in the proceedings.

For, at other times, the batter does not succeed, and his bat strikes the ball so viciously that the batted ball flies into an expanse of open space, and the fielders have to chase madly for it, as if possessed.

But the fielder is not the only one behaving frantically. The batter is running as if pursued by devils from one base (again, counterclockwise!) to the next. How he decides where to stop is unclear, but sometimes he apparently decides wrongly, and a referee announces loudly "You're out."

Thus, despite his best running efforts, or perhaps because of his excessive efforts, he also must leave the game. This repetitious pattern - one out, two out, three outs - over and over - must mean there is a huge assortment of men who assemble for the sport. Apparently, about 30 to 40 players take part in a single game for each team. There doesn't seem to be space on each bench for that many bodies. However, no doubt extra players enter the game through dark hallways near the benches. These tunneled halls apparently lead elsewhere in the stadium. Perhaps they use volunteers from the audience, providing they have brought the correct uniforms.

After both teams have had nine turns at both offense and defense, one team is declared the winner, retires peacefully, while members of the losing team walk past each other in a long double line, slapping hands and promising each other to do better next time.

Now, that is all that I am able to say without having my own qi revolt on me. The American tendencies toward anger and wrong-headedness are all too apparent in this sport. You should have no desire to learn it or ever attend a game.

I yearn for my return to our sensible and serene country. Remember to keep my spot warm at the backgammon table.

SUMMER EXPECTATIONS

By: Virginia Coleman

The summer after my high school graduation, I worked as a salesperson in a local dress shop. My parents were moving yet again and I was determined to spend the summer before college in the town I loved among people I knew. My job was a way for me to declare my independence and control my own life, which I expected to be calm, following a daily routine in familiar surroundings.

I roomed with an older woman who was kind - but loved to talk. I think she rented the room in order to have someone around to listen to her daily tales and gossip. My room was attractive with large windows that overlooked the formal garden next door and usually let in a cool breeze. A lovely serene blue covered the walls.

Work at the dress shop was leisurely as it stocked higher-priced ladies wear and was not as busy as some of the local stores. The owner liked to leave early on summer afternoons so I was frequently there alone. Pleased that she had confidence in my ability to work alone. I did not want to disappoint her.

Breakfast and dinner at a small restaurant nearby where I could choose my own time and menu gave me the feeling of being adult and in control. I still visited with my old friends, attended the same church, and knew people on the street. My life was safe, orderly and pleasant - just as I had envisioned.

On a warm, sunny morning I prepared to walk downtown to eat and then work the afternoon hours at the shop when the birdsongs of the garden were interrupted by a loud noise as the whole house rattled and shook. The window glass vibrated and seemed likely to break from its frame. I ran downstairs, but my landlady was not to be found. I dashed to the house next door where my friend lived. Anna was as confused as I about what was going on. More loud booms, bangs, and pops were happening along with sirens and alarms sounding. Cars were speeding down the street with beeping horns and we could hear loud voices coming through the window screens.

We went to her front porch and saw people hurrying down the street as someone yelled, "The fireworks plant is exploding! Get out of here! The whole town can go up anytime!"

On the northern end of town was situated a plant which manufactured munitions and fireworks. It had been the scene of an explosion before and was held in trepidation by many people of the town.

Anna, her dog, and I joined the line of people rushing toward the bridge which would carry us across the river to safety - we hoped. As we turned onto the bridge, there was a constant stream of people. Mothers clutched babies and small children. Two ladies were in their bathrobes and slippers. An older woman was carrying a cat - which was giving good effort to escaping her arms. Older boys carried younger children on their shoulders as we all marched toward safety. As we fled, the town police cars and ambulances followed by fire and rescue trucks, sped into town.

People shouted, "Keep moving, keep moving," as we made our way across the bridge.

Bits of conversation flew between walkers. Some told of shattered windows, cracked walls, of dust, and flying debris, while others talked only of workers in the plant and if they could possibly have survived the terrible blasts.

An older man said, "If it gets to the underground magazine, the whole town will be destroyed."

We walked in fear and with prayer, relieved to be leaving our beautiful small town. When we reached the other side of the river, cars were parked everywhere as people were trying to check on loved ones. Only emergency vehicles were allowed on the bridge. Some of the drivers jumped from cars leaving doors open in their hurry to walk across the bridge into danger in order to rescue family and friends. Mass confusion abounded. There was an endless procession of people searching for family members. We connected with some of Anna's relatives and neighbors but continued to sit by the side of the road to watch the confusion, fright, and relief that played across the faces of our band of refugees.

Several hours later as I looked toward the road, I recognized my father's car. He was scanning faces as he drove and came to a stop when he saw mine.

"Come on. I've come to take you home," he said.

When I returned two days later it was like entering a war zone. National Guardsmen were on the streets. Shattered windows had been covered by tarps and boards, until the glass could be replaced. A feeling of disbelief hung over the town. Relieved that the town still stood and could be repaired, the people of the community drew together to mourn those who had been lost and to help survivors put their lives back together.

My desire to control my world and insure a calm, orderly routine had been disrupted by the reality of life.

FREE WRITING

By: Alice C. Cory

Free writing is a fun and effective way to break through writer's block and stir the creative juices. You set a certain amount of time aside (10, 15, 20 minutes) and write for that entire period of time. Keep your hand moving across the page or keyboard. If you get stuck, write about feeling stuck or simply continue writing the most recent word over and over until something comes to you.

Do not edit or evaluate as you go or be concerned with proper spelling or grammar. This is a free flow of thoughts, and it makes no difference if they are connected. Remember no one will see or read what you write unless you want to share. Writing without constraints of organization can lead to lively ideas and bursts of creativity. Write swiftly but stop abruptly at the end of the allocated time.

WRITTEN JULY 13, 2013 AFTER ATTENDING A QIGONG CONFERENCE:

Four days connecting with old friends, all involved at various levels in qigong. How long have I been part of this group? I've developed from being such a beginner that I hadn't begun yet to being quite proficient. Doesn't sound humble. Maybe doably proficient is more comfortable.

Chatter about so many things but the most fun was sharing tales and experiences with two women just discovering the beginning of their journey. Wide-eyed like children seeing something the first time, endless questions, same ahhs and ohhhs like children. Maybe each new opening within us is connecting with the childish sense of wonders. How incredible to fall back into something that still reaches that deep place.

How many more minutes?

Dinner will be late. Not sure what it will be: maybe BLT. Could have them every day. Yum
Good tomatoes are unknowable in winter. Stuck, stuck, stuck, stuck … oh, that's it …

The unknowables. So many so very much advanced; the founders, those who first discovered in a foreign land the unthinkables and unknowables that are now part of us, growing within our own culture. They scouted bravely, broke through barriers, financed those who couldn't speak English but could speak truths of the universe only imagined by those who sought.

Time has moved us through those barriers, broken through so much reluctance and disbelief and here we stand in a group of over hundreds of members with 250 attending an annual gathering, most greeting each other like old friends. Those old scouts of past times go in other directions that their daily experiences have taken them but it seems none leave the cores which they discovered and introduced all those decades ago. Awesome to chat with them. Awesome to chat. Awesome to chat. Awesome to chat.

One just returned from presentations in Columbia Maryland-one of the solid ones, grounded in incredible wisdoms who found himself from here to the Orient to the universe and back asking me where Chestertown is from Columbia. How funny is that. He pretends to be fearsome but there is deep softness within him. There has to be. He's brash but not really.

There is little doubt that human nakedness comes easily to him but not that of the personal. His biography weeped his uneasiness with the him he doesn't know, hasn't met, or has met and prefers to forget. When does he see his own greatness?

Times rippled through the four-day gathering. Times of the ancients around the edges whispering more secrets, the times of the 60s and 70s when these men ventured to learn the deep secrets and later joined by women doing the same. Women why so long? Times when the wise ones from far away were sponsored and brought to safety into our supposed First World Country. Times when the teachings in English started, times when the books were translated and published, times when those adventurous men seeking merely adventure returned home deciding it was more than an adventure.

Times that are here when we see them aging and we thirst to wring every word from them they haven't shared. Times when we are ready to strip our souls naked to become ensouled.

BROWNSVILLE CHRISTMAS

By: Larry Samuels

"Are we there yet?" I asked my mother. I was five years old. We were climbing the marble stairs in the interior of a very dark tenement apartment building in Brownsville, Brooklyn. It was 1955. She was holding my hand and the hand of my sister, who was three-and-a-half years old.

"Not yet," she said. By this time we were about on the second floor landing. "How about now?" when we had reached the third floor. "Soon," she answered. My sister wasn't talking, just climbing.

Finally, on the fourth floor, "Here we are!" she sang. It was slightly brighter up there. A weak stream of dusty light filtering down from the next landing up, at the roof door, compensated for the unlit light fixture mounted on the hall ceiling.

There was a zinc-coated metal milk box outside of the apartment as we approached the first door at the head of the stairs. I don't ever remember that we got milk, or anything else, delivered while we were living there, but most all of the apartment doors had milk boxes in front of them as well.

She unlocked the door and we stepped into a short foyer, as she turned on the wall switch. Walking down the foyer, we turned to the right into a large kitchen. She turned on the light in here and I saw the sink against a wall under a window, next to the stove, which was next to the refrigerator. A white-enameled metal table with four chairs around it occupied the center of this large room.

Mom said, "Go through that hall to your room." My sister and I ran through the kitchen, past the living room on the left, into a short hallway, past the bathroom on our right, to our room. A window without curtains let the sunlight onto our two beds placed catty-corner, with a dresser on one side of the room. I don't remember the move that day, nor do I remember my sister or I saying anything up to this point, but obviously our furniture had preceded us.

We were just moving from our small, but wonderful, two-story, six-room, wood-frame row house in Baisley Park, Queens. Besides a fleeting, very early memory of living in another apartment before my sister was born, the house in Baisley Park was about where my life began. This apartment living in Brooklyn was going to be different from the house, for sure.

So on this moving day, exploring our new apartment, my sister and I went over to the window in our room and looked out to the courtyard. The courtyard was a space between the sides of the rear elevations of four buildings, and we were looking out and down from the fourth floor.

Each apartment, all the way from our floor to the ground level, was connected by a clothesline from a place on the brick wall outside of one window, to a spot on the wall outside of a window of another apartment across the yard. Some of the clothes-lines were in use, loaded with laundry, held by wooden clothes pins, some of the lines were just sagging on their own. It was a long, long way down from each window to the courtyard floor.

Our replacement clothesline would be installed a few days later, with dad connecting it across the chasm with the help of a friend standing in an apartment across the way. Besides regular laundry, and how it was that we had a washing machine in that apartment I'm not too certain that I knew how we had one, but mom would later wash my favorite stuffed dog pet, Ruffy, and would hang him by his ears on that clothes-line–I was mortified! I had several stuffed animal pals, including a rabbit, whose name is outside of my memory, but Ruffy, a grey colored, well-worn, floppy-eared dog, was my favorite.

My sister and I left the bedroom, stepped into the hall and then to the living room. We looked over the top of the television set and through the two windows-they faced a narrow alley between another apartment building across from us, with more windows. Mom was now in the other bedroom, looking through a drawer in her dresser. Two divided light French doors separated our parent's room from the living room. I didn't think much of it at the time, but it was quite an elegant domicile for this part of Brooklyn.

Well, that's not entirely true. Unfortunately, when we went into the bathroom, it didn't even have a sink in there, only a bathtub and a toilet. Really, what were they thinking of when they built this place, probably pre-1917, before World War I. Well, there are plenty of worse apartment buildings in Brooklyn, so I know we had it good. The apartment was bright, freshly painted and otherwise comfortable.

This residence was located on Amboy Street, between Sutter and Blake Avenues. This was, and still is, in this second decade of the twenty-first century, a particularly rough and poverty-stricken area of Brooklyn, made famous in the trilogy of gang books written by Irving Shulman, "The Amboy Dukes," "Cry Tough," and "The Big Brokers." The first book introduces the Dukes, the second continues their saga in the neighborhood and the third chronicles the relocation by some of them to Las Vegas, Nevada, to establish the gambling casinos out there. All based on true stories.

These fellows were our neighbors. When we were living there, I remember so vividly seeing a bunch of them leaning on a car at the corner, dressed in leather jackets. They were no bother to us, though. In those days, everyone mostly left each other alone, unless there was some reason to be messing with someone, for personal or gang reasons –well, just like now.

This section of Brooklyn was also highlighted in the 1949 film, "City Across the River," based on Shulman's first book, with a young Tony Curtis playing the part of one of the Dukes, Thelma Ritter playing a very tired, worn-out mother, and the story involving the murder of a high school shop teacher.

Brownsville is also well-known for the organization known as Murder, Inc., a very enterprising business idea in its time during the 1920s – 1940s, providing contract killing as needed, upon which the book and a 1960 movie are based. A good part of this history, however, was just about ending when we were living there. But it was really close.

I lost Santa Claus in that apartment on Amboy Street. For a long time, I had been saying to mom and dad that what I wanted for Christmas was a boat that sinks. What I saw in my mind was something like a pirate ship or one of Christopher Columbus's ships, or the Mayflower, with a little hatch on the side that I could open to let the water in, sinking it while taking a bath.

This particular Christmas eve I stayed up as late as I could, with all of my six stuffed animals, including Ruffy, resting with me on my pillow, hoping that Santa would walk right into the room that I shared with my sister. Even while trying to keep at least one eye open, I fell asleep before he got there, just like I had done the year before.

Christmas morning came, my sister and I ran out of our room into the kitchen where all of the presents were. I opened one box and found–a submarine. I knew in crystal clarity at that immediate moment that Santa Claus could not have made that mistake; it must have been my parents. There was no Santa Claus for me again after that.

Except that he came back one more time many years later. I was celebrating my first Christmas with my wife's family, before we were married, sleeping over at her sister's house in Connecticut. We had been together for seven months, to be married the following year, and now for more than twenty-five years. I was not any young age at the time of this Christmas: I was actually thirty-five.

Christmas morning came and we were all opening presents. My wife's parents, her brother, her sister and brother-in-law, and our nieces were there. I was handed a nicely wrapped package and looked at the tag, "To a Wonderful Son, from Santa," written in my future mother-in-law's handwriting, although I didn't immediately seem to recognize it. For the very briefest of microseconds I had this vision, this confusion, how could Santa be giving me a present?

I was back in the days of my childhood for that one fleeting moment. What an overwhelming feeling can be generated from the power of the mind. It was very mystical and quite unsettling. I quickly re-focused and opened the gift, a beautiful book on steam trains. I laughed and thanked my mother-in-law. I remember the completely magical feeling of that moment.

It's like when my daughter, at age nine, told us that she had already figured out that the tooth fairy was not real. She said that she had known the tooth fairy wasn't coming around, even though she continued to let us put the tooth under her pillow and then we replaced it with a quarter when she had fallen asleep. She never woke up while we were doing this. I still have most of her baby teeth, and our son's as well. This time of change when she gave up the tooth fairy was a very sad moment for me.

Maybe not as bad though, since she had already told us about the tooth fairy, was about the same time when she told us that she did not believe in Santa Clause anymore.

Up until that time, we had still been placing a cookie and a glass of milk near the Christmas tree. After she fell asleep, we would take a bite out of the cookie and would spill out some of the milk. We enjoyed doing that. She didn't let on that it was over until at least two years running that we were still doing this. I can't recall the circumstances of how we learned that our son had stopped believing in the tooth fairy and Santa Clause, but he must have been about the same age, or younger. Although it's inevitable that children lose their belief in these things, it's a hard road for the parents. Well, it was for me anyway.

Maybe it's not as hard for a child when they're going through that loss, maybe it's not so traumatic. Maybe they just glide through it peacefully while it happens, maybe not. It didn't slide past me that easily that morning on Amboy Street. I clearly remember the moment of accepting such truth when I opened that submarine – it was a hard truth for me. I am now, as I remember how I lost that belief, as melancholy as I was then about Christmas in Brownsville. I keep that feeling handy –it reminds me to celebrate the mystery of belief.

MY DAD
A Father's Day Remembrance
By: Susan Brittain

This story begins with a Marriage certificate dated March 22nd 1870. George Brittain, Shipwright, marries Ann Williams, Spinster, at St. Nicholas Church in Liverpool, England. That's the earliest recorded document of my family. From this wonderful union, two generations and 49 years later my father was born in Leytonstone, a borough of East London, within the sound of Bow Bells Church, immediately making him a true cockney.

Reginald, my father, was a twin, born first, the strongest and the most likely to succeed. He was followed an hour or so later by Ronald, his brother.

His father, my grandfather, had emerged from the horror of World War 1 (and losing his two brothers) only because he had served as an Ambulance Corps driver. A nightmare he never brought up in conversation. I know little about my father's childhood except that he had a father and mother who rode motorcycles and who were very much in love. His mother Flo died when she was fifty from cancer. I would hear brief mentions of camping and rowing at a small summer coastal town called Mayland-on-Sea, playing amateur football (or soccer as you Yanks seem to prefer), the pride of a father who did the books for London transport.

He was accepted into the University of London

where he studied the sciences, but in 1939 was evacuated out of London and moved to the University of Cambridge with the start of World War II. On finishing his degree in 1942 he went to war serving in the Special Forces and taking part in the D-Day landings. Just like his father he never once mentioned one battle or skirmish that he faced during that time.

The end of World War II found him a rising star in the military working for the Ministry of Defense as a weapons specialist, selling arms to foreign nations. It was in this capacity that he was loaned to the US government and flown to Tokyo where working alongside Henry Kissinger he met a young American secretary recently discharged from the U.S. Navy. They were married on 20th of April 1952 in Washington, DC. He was 32, she 30. Reg and Corinne sailed back to England by steamship and in no time at all, four boys had joined the picture.

I don't think my father really ever knew what hit him but he tried his hardest to be a father. I always think of Mary Poppins and Mr. Banks singing the lines, "A British home is run with Tradition" except we never had a Mary Poppins to fix and organize our house. My dad caught a train to London every weekday morning and would return at 6:35 each evening, brief case and brolly in hand. He hoped to be greeted at the door by his loving wife with a Martini but it was usually with requests for homework help, fixing a bike, where does part #24 go on this Revel model plane and: I am not going to bed till after Dr. Who.

My father was good at marching us, and every Saturday we would set out along the River Wey tow path, leaving my mother to scale and conquer the Mount Everest of laundry we had scattered throughout the house over the previous week. And then, like the artist Cristo, she would decorate our back yard with clothes, sheets and towels in collages of colors be it winter or summer.

These walks down the towpath would be a test of endurance and discipline for us. No running ahead, no hands in pockets, no throwing stones, no splashing and no physical contact. I think the first infraction always occurred about 10 seconds into our walk and didn't stop until we reached the little ice cream store where airs and graces were put on full display by the most beautiful four boys ever to grace this planet. Then fueled by chocolate and ice cream we returned home punching, kicking and running, leaving my father to ponder that the D-Day landings had been more successful than his assault on the ice cream store.

My father loved Christmas. The tree, the decorations, the presents. It was at Christmas us boys would try really hard to be good but one of us just had to be bad for the rest to follow. It was just too tempting to grab a broom and knock down paper chains, decorations and ornaments.

.   There was always the Kings College choir Christmas carols, on an LP removed from its sleeve and dusted off with reverence each Christmas Eve. For peanuts and a tiny bottle of soda us boys would sing Christmas carols. Smirking, fidgeting, and with no sense of the holy night, we would wait for Father Christmas.

It always seemed that our turkeys never wanted to cook themselves and, like surgeons working frantically over a patient, my parents would work with that Turkey for hours and hours until magically at 6 p.m. on Christmas day we would sit at the grand table in the dining room that was always forbidden territory the rest of the year.

We pulled on Crackers to extract little toys, and paper hats to put on. Spooned through plum pudding to find a hidden sixpence and always managed to spill something. My father, as the Martini's and wine took effect, gave us long lectures about how he couldn't afford this and we were going to be in the poor house by January.

Then it was off to bed and of course an hour later the obligatory, " If I have to come up there, there will be hell to pay," which really meant we could keep hitting each other and jumping on the bed for at least another half hour.

Summers were spent on the East coast of England in a little cottage called Averest, a cockney play on words. The day school ended was spent in frenzied packing and organizing and the next morning we would be off through London to the Essex marshes and paradise.

Report cards and school were quite forgotten. The greatest gift my father gave me was his love of the water. Our summers were spent racing sailboats, swimming and exploring the creeks and estuaries of the River Blackwater.

On race days my father would pace the shore line, waiting for the lead boat to round a mark and see the green and purple spinnaker go up and knew I was leading, be it in a fleet of 10 or 200. I knew he would be smiling and would have bragging rights at the Yacht Club bar. This was a carefree life that no longer exists and one I have always yearned to go back to.

As I grew, life's problems pushed us apart. I dropped out of college, a double-edged sword, for I had just won the British University Sailing Team championship.

I dug my heels in at career choices and refused to further my life's goals. I left for America at 23 and became what he used to term a "Boat Bum." He was the first in his family to go to college, to succeed, to send his children to private schools and all he wanted was a better life for us. But I wanted none of it. I was of the 70s generation of hitch hiking and cheap travel.

I could have written about the father that couldn't call to say hello, the father who missed my wedding, and never knew his grandson, but I have come to realize that his generation was just never taught to do these things.

They grew up between two world wars, in the Great Depression and had never seen men pick up children, hug them, bathe them, change their diapers and blow their noses. His job was to provide for the family and take care of R and R.

I sat next to him when he took his last breath in September of 1997, and a week later we motored down his favorite river in the Yacht Club launch and scattered his ashes at the Club's finish line. Of course he was the first to do this.

How will my son in thirty years write about me on Father's Day? Will my story bear the testament of time, and will my son be strong enough to tell it?

NOTHING TO FIND

By: Marguerite Anne Samuels

Ben figured the police would be looking for a fourteen-year-old boy with curly brown hair: about five foot four. But he wasn't going to stop, not until he found a man named Russ Graham. Three bus rides were a long way from Bridgeton, New Jersey; however, Ben wanted to find the man who had left him at The Home for Boys eleven years ago.

The fumes bothered Ben. He rolled up the sleeves of an oversized Army jacket. Then he opened the window, caught a sign, "Albany 10 miles" and took pretzels out of his knapsack.

"He told me to give this to you when you were old enough to understand who he was," Reverend Peterson had said when he gave him his father's jacket about a year ago.

He reached into his pocket and took out the photo he had discovered. Ben turned it over and looked again at the information penciled on the back. Rughide, N.Y. Russ Graham. All he had ever shared with his father was a name. Ben flipped the photo over and stared at the image. Like Ben, this man had curly brown hair, brown eyes, and thick eyebrows. In this picture, this man appeared to be about thirty years old. He also had a mustache and goatee and dark circles around his eyes. How could Ben speak to him? Reverend Peterson was more like a father to Ben than this stranger in the photo, but yet, this was *his* father; there was no denying the resemblance.

Ben felt a cramp, stretched his leg and kicked the seat in front of him. A woman turned around, snapped gum, and said, "Watch it, will ya?"

She looked like one of those people whose picture belonged in a new wallet whenever he bought one. Ben could make sense of the world by reducing people to wallet size photos that belonged somewhere. But he couldn't do that with his father. He couldn't place his father's photo anywhere.

When the bus pulled into the Albany Bus Terminal, Ben got off. He knew from the map that Rughide was five miles to the west. He began walking in the direction of the setting sun. He figured he would arrive in Rughide about 6:30 p.m.

Ben passed gas stations, used car lots, and bars until he was out of Albany. The exercise felt good to him. A few houses were built like jack-o-lanterns and a deer leapt across the road. Several cars passed him.

The Rughide Bar 'N Grill was the first sign of the town. Ben passed several guys hanging out on the tail of a pick-up truck. He walked farther up the road and came to the Rughide Market.

Ben entered the grocery store, picked up an apple, and bit into it.

"Hey, what do you think you're doing?"

Ben noticed a man hustling behind him to reach for the apple in his hand. He was wearing a flannel shirt that was covered with a stained white apron.

"Good apple, mister," Ben said.

"Thirty-five cents," the man said. He held out his right hand, which was missing the pinky finger.

Ben ate a few more bites of the apple, took out a quarter and a dime to hand the man, and then pulled out the photo.

"Ever seen him before?" Ben asked.

The storeowner glanced at the photo quickly, shrugged his shoulders, and grimaced. He raised his bushy eyebrows and said, "Don't know the man. Should I?"

Then he sauntered toward the cash register. Ben followed him and quickened his pace.

"Russ Graham," Ben said. He threw the photo on the moving checkout belt.

"Fifty cents," the storeowner said. He picked up the photo and placed it in a small brown bag.

Ben banged his left fist on the counter, took out the photo, and repeated the name "Russ Graham."

The storeowner shook his head and said, "The name doesn't ring a bell."

Ben picked up the photo. Then he saw a pay phone with some directories.

"If you're looking for trouble . . ."

"The apple's paid for."

Ben walked over to the directories and looked up "Graham," but none were listed.

"Store's closing." The storeowner cleared his throat.

Ben grabbed the Yellow Pages directory, looked under cemeteries, and memorized some of their addresses.

He took a few more bites of the red delicious apple, threw the core into the trash basket near the checkout counter, and left the store.

The sky was twilight blue which meant he could still read the gravestones if he hurried. One cemetery was up the road. He looked down each row. No Russ Graham. As he was leaving, he saw headlights.

"I'm Officer Michaels. I got a call from the grocer who told us you might be in some kind of trouble." Officer Michaels was a heavyset cop with a robust chest and large nose.

Ben turned around and noticed that his partner was sitting at the wheel of the patrol car. His right hand fidgeted in his pocket.

"What were you looking for?" Officer Michaels asked. His breath smelled of garlic and onions.

"Nothing." Ben took his hand out of his pocket and Officer Michaels quickly put his one hand on his gun. Then Ben began to run.

Ben heard the patrol car screeching, the sound moving closer to him, the headlights invading his space.

Then Ben heard footsteps. Officer Michaels caught up with him. "We just called Albany and they heard from the New Jersey State Police. Reverend Peterson reported you missing. Ben Graham, right?"

"So, what if that is my name? What it's to anyone?" Ben tried to run again, but Officer Michaels grabbed him.

"Reverend Peterson wired the money. My duty is to take you back to Albany and put you on a bus and ride with you on that bus until I return you to your home safely," Officer Michaels said.

Ben pushed him away. Then he began running again. The patrol car followed him. Officer Michaels pursued Ben, reached for him, and caused him to trip by throwing his stick down on the ground.

"Get in the car now," Officer Michaels said.

"You don't understand. No one understands. I've got to find my father, my real father."

"If I were on a road hundreds of miles from my home looking for my father, I wouldn't call him my father," Officer Michaels said.

Ben held his jacket. "This is his jacket. He wanted me to have this, so I could understand who he is . . ."

"He is a victim like you are, like my son was . . . " Officer Michaels looked at Ben and threw his arm around him.

Ben drew closer to him and asked, "Why? Why did my father leave me?"

"Some questions don't have answers. "

Ben picked up a stone and threw it. "Reverend Peterson gave me this jacket. It had a picture of my father. His name is penciled on the back of the photo with the name of this town. I just thought . . ."

Ben hung his head. The officer then got up and opened the car door.

Ben moved toward the car and got in. Officer Michaels closed the door, ran to the other side, and jumped in the front seat.

Officer Michaels checked his watch. "Jerry, we've got time. Let's drive Ben to the other cemetery."

When they arrived at the Rughide Cemetery, Officer Michaels handed Ben a flashlight and said, "Take your time." Then he placed a hand on Ben's shoulder and sighed.

Ben walked through each row, looked at every gravestone, but none were marked "Russ Graham." Then he sat on a gravestone. *There was nothing to find in this town.*

Ben looked at the sky. The same stars he saw Reverend Peterson would be viewing through his telescope because he liked Astronomy. He remembered what Reverend Peterson always said about God, the Father. Ben always wondered why Reverend Peterson quoted Psalm 147: 4 "He counts the number of stars; He gives names to all of them" until now. He realized where he belonged. Ben took out the photo, placed it in his wallet, and returned to the patrol car.

"Any luck, son?" Officer Michaels asked. He was snacking on some potato chips and a soda.

Ben shook his head.

"Sorry, kid."

Ben took out his wallet. "Can I show you a picture of my father?"

Officer Michaels looked at the picture. "He's a hero in a different sense. Maybe he didn't raise you, but he made sure you had a nice home and were taken care of by Reverend Peterson."

"I'm done here," Ben said.

In an hour, Ben was sitting next to Officer Michaels on a bus headed from Albany, New York to Bridgeton, New Jersey. Officer Michaels was dozing while saliva was staining his blue shirt. Ben wondered if Reverend Peterson wouldn't mind asking God to name a star "Graham" for his father, wherever he was, but at least, he would then have something to find through a telescope. He also found something else–people who cared about him and where he was headed.

CANCUN CALLING

By: Alice Lindsay

The return address on the envelope reads: Mexico Money Gram Transfer, PO Box 1000, Mexico City, Mexico. I figure it's just another travel promo and toss it aside to get to the more meaty mail—the monthly bills. But then the thought of Tim's spring break in Cancun pops into my mind. Tim is our son. It was 1993. He was a sophomore at Dickinson College. Sipping my morning coffee, I smile and remember...

That snapshot of Tim on the beach in the lineup of college buddies--five big bruisers with broad shoulders, wash board abs and black chest hair—Tim on the end of the line, the skinny blonde kid half hidden behind the Charles Atlas with a beard. I smile again. But then reality sets in as I remember all those collect phone calls starting with that one from college...

"Mom, this is Tim."

"Yes, I know your voice, Sweetie. What's up? I have no money."

"Mom, spring break starts in three weeks. All the guys are going to Cancun for a week. Can't I go? Awww! Please, Mom?"

"I said I have no money."

"Awww! Mom. It's not all that much. And I'll save up all of my allowance 'til then.

"It's probably all spent already. But what about your grades? You need that time to catch up for finals.

At least that's what you said."

"Awww! Mom. I'll come home every weekend to study… after vacation…I promise…I'll even…"

Promises, promises, and I ended up promising to take the matter up with his father, that putty-in-Tim's-hands man. Dan, of course, could find no telling argument against the Cancun caper. I saw nothing but trouble, not to mention expense, but gave the final go-ahead. The check was mailed, the travel arrangements made, and Tim was set for his first venture off U.S. soil, his second air trip. Departure day came, but so did another phone call:

"Hello, Mom. It's Tim."

"Yes, I know. Now what?"

"Mom, I'm at the airport."

"So…bon voyage!"

"Mom, the plane is leaving in half an hour."

"Yes…?"

"I have to get on the plane."

"That might be a start."

"Mom, I can't."

"What!"

"I'm too scared to fly."

"Tim, you've been all through that with Dr. Smith. You know what to do: the relaxation, the deep breathing, the imaging, the revised thoughts, the whole cognitive/behavioral program."

Silence.

"Tim…are you still there?"

"…Yes…"

"Well?"

"I'm scared."

"I know. But I thought you wanted to vacation with the guys."

220

"I did, but..."

"'But', nothing. Get on the damn plane! Do the program."

Silence

"Tim?"

"...All right...OK...I'll go...But...

" No 'buts.' We love you. Dad says 'good-bye.' Have a great time."

There were no reports of air crashes for the duration of Tim's flight. As a "Fly without Fear Therapy" dropout and a strictly white knuckled flyer myself, I was relieved. And I was pretty much succeeding in putting students-on-vacation images of shark attacks, muggings, drunken brawls and infectious sexual encounters out of my mind when once again—the phone. Nine p.m. and just two days into the dream vacation with all the guys. I pick up the phone

"Hello...Hello...?

"Hello...Mom..."

"Tim...Are you all right? What's wrong?"

"I think I'm having a heart attack!"

"You're, *what*?"

"My chest hurts, and my heart is going a mile a minute. Mom, I'm scared."

"You're nuts! You're twenty years old, you just passed a physical with flying colors, and there's absolutely no heart trouble in this family."

"But, Mom..."

"You're having another panic attack," I say, hoping I'm sounding matter-of-fact.

"No, Mom, I think I'm dying."

"No, you aren't. Now listen to me. Just to put your mind at rest, call the desk and tell whoever answers that you need to see a doctor right away, that you're having serious chest pains. They have doctors down there, don't they?"

"I guess so."

"Call the desk, now! And call me back."

Tim didn't. Naturally I was tempted to call him, but decided that not showing concern was the better course to follow. So instead I spent all night indulging in worst-case scenarios. I guess I got a little sleep until the phone rang around 8 o'clock.

"Mom, this is Tim."

"Well, you're sounding better. Did you see a doctor?"

"Yes, Dr. Labenga came to my room about a half hour after we talked."

""Dr. Labenga? Hmmm… The name has a certain musical quality to it."

"Well, he could pass for a disco dancer. He was wearing a skintight red silk shirt open to the belly button over tight white pants and dripping with gold chains."

"Colorful! And what did he do?"

"Well, he was dragging the hotel EKG machine right behind him, so he gave me an EKG test right off. Right here in my room.

"A hotel EKG machine! What will they think of next! And, what did the test show?"

"It was normal."

"Of course," I said, suppressing a sigh of relief…."And?"

"And he gave me a shot of Valium in my rear end to relax."

"And…"

"And I went to sleep and slept all night."

"So, it wasn't a heart attack after all."

"I guess not."

"Well, that's good. So what do you plan to do today?"

"I think I'll just stay in my room and watch TV." *You had to go all the way to Mexico to do that,* I thought.

We said our "Love ya's!" and "good-byes."
With only three days left to Tim's vacation—or perhaps, better, his rest cure—I remember thinking that would be the end of the phone calls. But it took just one day before his return trip to scotch that fantasy.

"Mom, it's Tim."

"I know, dear. Is everything all right?"

`"Well, yes and no."

"Let's hear the 'no' part."

"I have to pay Dr. Labenga's bill, and I don't have enough money left. Could you wire me some? Please?"

"You can't check out of the hotel without paying and then send the money later? So I have to go to the trouble of wiring it right now? I have a million things to do today?"

"Well, the hotel manager said I have to pay now."

"He would. But I guess it figures. So, how much?"

"It's $100 for Dr. Labenga and $55 for the EKG machine, including the test. That comes to $155.

"Yes, I can add. Well, I'm relieved Mexican medical fees are so reasonable."

"Will you send it right away?"

I sigh. "Of course. What's the address and to whom do I send it?"

I jot down the info. Tim is all "thanks" and "love

ya's!" He promises not to have a panic attack on the flight home. We say our "good-byes." I wire the cash and start worrying his plane might crash.

Tim got home safe and sound. More cognitive therapy and discovering a life purpose in becoming a physical therapist got him over his panic attacks. Swearing off spring break and other college party boozing didn't hurt either.

The astronomical phone bill that arrived a month after Tim returned gave his father a mental fit bordering on planned child abuse. I reminded him of his complicity in the Cancun caper. But he picked up the phone anyway, and put in a call to Tim at school—long distance, of course—to chew him out.

That was a laugh. When I quit listening and left the room, they were reminiscing about our last fishing trip to Deep Creek Lake the summer before and planning another. Only the "Hello, Tim?" had sounded the least bit gruff.

I finish my coffee and am about to get on with paying the bills, when the envelope from Mexico again catches my eye. I decide to open it. Inside I find a notice entitled, "Mexico Money Transfer Litigation Settlement." It's telling me about the successful class action suit brought on behalf of persons who used Money Gram Transfer Service, as I had, to wire money from anywhere in the U.S. to Mexico between January, 1988 and August, 1999. Those falling under the settlement are entitled to coupons for discounts on any future money transfers to Mexico. I'm thinking, *Just what I need, discount coupons for wiring money to Mexico!* But then I realize no such luck. A closer reading of the legalese reveals that during the eligibility time period, computer records showed I made only one money transfer. To receive any coupons I would have had to have made ten. Who, I wonder, besides a drug dealer makes ten money transfers to Mexico in a lifetime? Okay, so maybe an employed immigrant supporting a family back home.

Taking my failure to qualify for the coupon freebie in philosophical stride, I toss the money transfer notice in the trash with the rest of the junk mail. Then I consider how lucky I really am. After all, it wasn't a heart attack, and only one of those calls from Cancun asked for money.

I just hope Dr. Labenga didn't waste any of my money buying red silk shirts slashed to the navel, tight white pants and gold chains.

SNIPPETS

MUCH THE SAME
By: Nancy McCloy

"Get off the floor. I said, GET OFF the FLOOR, fix your face, and go back into the dining room."

Quickly rising, Jeannette got up, dabbed at her eyes and headed in the direction of the dining room. A few faces inquired after her then quickly, carelessly returned to their drinks, the dinner, the person, and the thoughts that more interested them than she. She didn't belong here anyways. Not like they did.

"What was I thinking, bringing her here? Too soon. Way too soon. You just don't bring a 10-year-old diva to a very expensive French restaurant, even if it was to celebrate her lead role in a dance recital. Especially when this diva had demanded to go to Pizza Palace and she usually—well always—got her way. NOT today; hence the major public meltdown.

"What was I thinking? Why would I be surprised? Hmm. Got it!"

Like mother, like daughter.

NIGHT LIGHT
By: Larry Samuels

Night creeps,
Night runs
Showing setting suns

Light fades,
Light recedes
While the moon now leads

Dark piercing,
Dark sprinkling
With the stars twinkling

Until on morning,
Until night lifts
Its presence as old gifts

SWAN SONG
By: Frances Reed

The piano was magnificent.

"Buy me a grand piano" she'd wheedled. "I've always wanted a grand piano!"

Doug loved his wife. So here it sat, in all its expensive glory. His present to his new wife: a luminous, white, baby grand.

He ran his fingers over the keys and picked out "Happy Birthday." Smiling, he envisioned Leanne's delight.

She was coming…

She was here.

"So, Honey," he asked, filled with pride at his cleverness and generosity, "how do you like it?"

She walked around the piano trailing her manicured fingers along its shiny surface and then turned to face him. He waited eagerly for her accolades.

"It's the wrong color." She said.

NIGHT SHIFT
By: Nancy McCloy

The night shift is not so bad.
You get to have lunch at 3 in the morning then breakfast for dinner and sleep when most poor souls are revving their engines for another daily grind of carpools, commuting to work during rush hour, or trying, yet again, to find a decent job.
You get to avoid most things that go bump in the night. You know, those memories, sounds, and images that stalk like a panther, making sweet dreams impossible.
Nothing seems nearly so bad in the dawn of a new day, spread before you with infinite options and possibilities. Life is good or not nearly as bad as it seems during a stretch of night insomnia or nightmares.
Yeah, the night shift isn't so bad.
The only thing better would be if I got on the day shift.

WORDS
By: Joe Cullis

Why do I use simple words when I write?
Because words are like things we do in
Our lives and if we fill our minds with too
Many big ones we tend to forget the joy that
The simple and little things can give us.

****

This is an excerpt from one of my works in progress.
Working Title- Twil'it
Science Fiction Fantasy
Joe Cullis

A tribe of ancient beings gathered around a great river. This river was not young; it had already carved deep gorges in the mountains from which it rose. However, compared to these beings, the mountains themselves were young. This is why the ancient ones came to this place.

The young mountains were only scarcely populated with life. The scattered areas where the rocks had eroded into a heavy soil were not completely covered by small plants. Genetically the plants were mostly the same. The amount of light caused some color changes and the varying heaviness of the soils caused some size differences. This gave the appearance of diversity, but in this relatively young world differences were still mostly superficial.

231

The potential for change at a rudimentary level was great. These ancient beings knew how to turn this potential into reality. It was their intent to do so. This is why they have come to this place.

WEEPING WILLOW
By: Marguerite Anne Samuels

Weep,
oh, weep no more, love
embraces evermore,
willow and wind console —the elongated leaves touch
me, branches lolling,
gentle dance, lifting
to heaven
willow and wind, wind and willow, clasping
closeness, willow branches dancing,
living, joy
and sorrow, sorrow and joy, tomorrow and today, today
and tomorrow, revealing
truth, rings circling,
aging, but not
dying,
alone, but not
lonely.
Remembering another
beneath the shadow of the elongated leaves pirouetting,
silhouetting our love, death a shadow, willow weep
no more.

FOUR BEFORE ONE

By: Larry Samuels

Does R22 refrigerant boil at 54°? Adding 22° to 0° Centigrade is 32° Fahrenheit, and gets you to 54°. Is R22 that number to match its boiling point, or maybe its cosmic weight?

I used to know lots of numbers. A cubic foot of water - 8.33 gallons; the boiling point of water - 212° at sea level; the speed of light - 186,000 miles per second.

I could only keep certain facts handy after Cynthia left. It had been me, and Cynthia, and Jayne, and Tom, four of us, a family. There are other numbers in families. Two is the minimum: one is not. One is a person.

Only three of us were happy. Me, Jayne and Tom. Then, as John Updike writes, *"Like pale slices of days darkening to a fatal shade,"* happiness for us slipped away.

Together for fifteen years, then gone, taking the children. I didn't see it coming. I played with them; I listened to her. Sometimes I was quiet. Sometimes I spoke up, like when I said she couldn't go to the movies with a friend. Supper wasn't ready; clothes needed washing; there were any number of things to do.

Or when she wanted me to bring the children to school at 8:00 a.m., even though she could have taken them on her way to a doctor's appointment. After all, I had to meet Jackson to go to the track. We needed to make the first race at 1:00 p.m. so I could bet the $100 dollars in my pocket. I couldn't be late, so she had to take the children. This was just the way it needed to be for the four of us.

She did take the children, away, and that was twelve days later. Too many numbers.

DOWNSIZING?

By: Alice Cory

Could I really live in 250 'eco-friendly' square feet? I wonder, peering at the stacks of books growing up from the basement floor; each teetering pile representing a life stage. Instead of generations of photo albums, I have tomes of reading material to mark my growing pains.

One pile to my left is from my late-twenties into thirties' "searching for myself through self-improvement" phase. It's possible that the greatest improvement may have been to the authors' wallets.

The middle stack, threatening to lean into the third grouping of cookbooks, is my "crash the corporate glass ceiling" stash with its subset of "effective business communication" resting nearby. "The glass ceiling was opaque enough to hide the next glass ceiling," I mumble as I turn to the remaining volumes awaiting their rightful placement in my latest organizational attempt. *I wonder if they even apply in today's world, what with Skyping and emailing and who knows what else?*

With this thought of changing times, I see myself in one of the new environmentally appropriate mini-houses, neat and efficient, but it seems oddly empty...no crafts, no books, no much-of-cluttered-anything.

"Ah-HA!" I shout while knocking over my "safe foraging in your backyard" grouping. TWO of those mini-houses; *that's* the answer...one, of course, for books.

CONTRIBUTORS

RONNY ASELTINE: Is a former member of a radical knitting group, sworn to secrecy and therefore cannot disclose any details of her current life. *(Find her on pages 37 and 111)*

SUSAN BRITTAIN: Has lived on 2 continents, in two Genders and sailed the oceans. She lives with her soul mate Cindy in a Purple Cottage in Chestertown. *(Find her on pages 77, 83 and 207)*

VIRGINIA COLEMAN: Retired, native of the Eastern Shore who admires a well turned phrase and creative people who labor with word and mood. *(Find her on pages 33,103,135 and 191)*

ALICE CORY: Is outside playing and will get back to you once she grows up. *(Find her on pages 5,121,195 and 236)*

JOSEPH C. CULLIS: Sitting down and writing is one of the hardest things for me to do, but when my mind needs consoling paper is my trusted confidant and a pen is my lover. When we unite I find an ecstasy that no other can give. *(Find him on pages 27,129 and 231)*

BARBARA HARBESON: Over a decade of life in Chestertown, creating, cultivating friends. Writing, teaching, loving, involved. *(Find her on pages 89 and 181)*

NANCY HARTMAN: Born and raised in Baltimore; has history and paralegal degrees; lives in Chestertown. *(Find her on pages 73 and 159)*

PEGGY JAEGLY: An award-winning storyteller, in both fiction and nonfiction, who helps others become published authors with her instructional program WRITE YOUR BOOK. *(Find her on pages 67 and 147)*

ALICE LINDSAY: Retired social worker, animal welfare activist, fellowship librarian, humor writer. Married with one grown son and one gorgeous Lab/setter mix named Laddie. *(Find her on pages 1, 95 and 219)*

NANCY MCCLOY: Wife, family member, friend, educator, community helper. Writing allows me to express these and the hidden "More." I write to discover me and, hopefully, you. *(Find her on pages 25, 227 and 230)*

AMETHYST MCNABB: Is discovering her voice after 25 years behind a microphone (*Find her on page 43*)

FRANCES REED: Divorced herself from Big Business several years ago and is now bigamously married to her writing and her Vintage Store in Chestertown MD. *(Find her on pages 53,139, 183 and 229)*

MARGUERITE ANNE SAMUELS: Residing in Chestertown, Maryland with her husband, Larry and their two children Paul and Rebecca. Marguerite is an adjunct professor in English *(Find her on page 213 and 233)*

LARRY SAMUELS: Raised in Brooklyn, New York, served as Petty Officer in U.S. Navy during Vietnam, lives in Chestertown, Maryland with wife Marguerite and children, Paul and Rebecca. *(Find him on pages 57, 163,199 228 and 236)*

LINDA WEIMER: Is a retired newspaper and magazine reporter. She lives in Chester Harbor, just outside Chestertown. *(Find her on pages 13, 107, 155 and 187)*

www.ingramcontent.com/pod-product-compliance
Lightning Source LLC
Chambersburg PA
CBHW072220170626
46813CB00003B/1030